# AVIATION

A REFERENCE
FIRST BOOK

**BY GILDA BERGER**

FRANKLIN WATTS
NEW YORK | LONDON | TORONTO
SYDNEY | 1983

Cover photographs courtesy of: Culver Pictures: top left; n.c.: top center; The Collection of the Library of Congress: top right; Zeppelin Museum, Freidrichshafen: bottom right; Federal Aviation Administration: bottom left; Boeing Airline Co.: middle left.

Photographs courtesy of:

U.S. Navy Photo Center: p. 4; Library of Congress: p. 9, 26, 60; French Embassy Press & Information Desk: p. 16; New York Public Library Picture Collection: pp. 17, 42, 51, 59, 79, 81, 88, 91; Official U.S. Air Force Photos: pp. 18, 54, 66, 77, 83, 89; U.S. Army Photograph: p. 22; Boeing Airline Company: pp. 24, 29; Cessna: p. 28; Carl Byoir & Associates: p. 31; Royal Air Force: p. 36; Federal Aviation Administration: p. 47; CIA: p. 62; Imperial War Museum: p. 76 (both)

Library of Congress Cataloging in Publication Data

Berger, Gilda.
Aviation.

(A Reference first book)
Summary: Presents alphabetically arranged
definitions of terms, physical principles, people,
and organizations having to do with aviation.
Also identifies types of aircraft.
1. Aeronautics—Dictionaries, Juvenile.
[1. Aeronautics—Dictionaries] I. Title. II. Series.
TL509.B39  1983    629.13'003'21    83-3682
ISBN 0-531-04645-1

# AVIATION

**A-1.** *See* DOUGLAS A-1.

**ACE.** The name given to a pilot who shoots down large numbers of enemy aircraft. According to U.S. military custom, one witness must see the plane crash or explode before it is counted as a kill (aircraft shot down). A film of the hit may also count. Since it is often difficult to count planes that have crashed out of sight or in the heat of battle, the actual number of planes shot down by war aces is probably higher than the records show.

During World War I the French were the first to apply the title "ace" to any pilot who shot down five enemy planes. The French ace René Fonck (1894–1953) shot down seventy-five planes; another Frenchman, Georges Guynemer (1894–1917), destroyed fifty-four planes.

The most famous American World War I ace was Captain Eddie Rickenbacker (1890–1973), a former auto racer, who shot down twenty-two German planes and four balloons between April and November 1918.

Among the greatest fliers of all was Germany's Manfred Von Richthofen (1892–1918), known as the Red Baron, who shot down eighty planes before his death in April 1918.

Air power was used far more in World War II, and several World War I totals were topped. Major Richard Bong (1920–1945) of the U.S. Army Air Forces downed forty Japanese aircraft. Russia's best-known ace, Major Alexander Pokryshkin (b. 1913), destroyed fifty-nine German planes between 1941 and 1945.

**ADER, CLÉMENT** (1841–1925). A French electrical engineer and inventor who built a steam-powered airplane called *Éole* that looked like a bat but could not sustain flight. Ader took off in the craft on October 9, 1890, and flew 150 feet (46 m) before wrecking the aircraft. Another of his planes, the *Avion,* flew to a height of 60 feet (18.3 m) before coming down. Although plagued with failure, Ader is credited by some to be the first man in history to lift off the ground in a powered craft of his own design.

**AERIAL PHOTOGRAPHY.** The taking of photos from an airborne aircraft. The first known aerial photos were taken by Aime Laussedat in the late 1850s. He is called the "father of aerial photography." The first aerial photographs ever published were taken by a Frenchman, Gaspard Felix Tournachon (1820–1910), who called himself Nadar. Nadar photographed Paris in 1868 from a balloon tethered at 1,700 feet (518 m). During World War I aerial photography was sometimes used for military purposes. Subsequently it became a most important source of military intelligence in time of war and a tool for mapping in peacetime.

**AEROBATICS.** Precision flying or stunts performed during flight by an airplane, glider, or other similar aircraft. Aerobatic competitions resemble figure skating competitions in some ways.

**AEROBATS.** Planes that are used in competition. The aerobatic airplanes must perform standard maneuvers in a precise way. In some competitions the flyers are told the combinations of maneuvers well in advance. In some, the maneuvers are revealed shortly before flight. Still others leave the combinations up to the pilot.

**AERODYNAMICS.** The branch of study that deals with the flow of air around objects and with the effects of such motion on objects in air.

**AERONAUTICS.** The science and art of flight.

**AERONAUTS.** Name for pilots of balloons or other lighter-than-air aircraft.

**AERO SPACELINES B-377 "PREGNANT GUPPY."** An aircraft (1962) designed to transport large booster rockets and other items used in the U.S. space program. A huge "bubble" was built over the top of the fuselage, making the entire fuselage 19 feet 9 inches (6.02 m) wide. The tail was removable in order to allow straight-in loading of the booster rockets. When introduced, the B-377 had the largest cabin of any aircraft in the world. (Wingspan, 141 feet 3 inches [43 m]; length, 127 feet [39 m].)

**AEROSTAT.** Any lighter-than-air craft, such as a balloon or dirigible.

**AICHI TYPE 99 "THE VAL."** The Japanese dive bomber, launched from an aircraft carrier, that took part in the surprise attack on the U.S. military naval station at Pearl Harbor on December 7, 1941. Twenty-five Vals, led by Lt. Akira Sakamoto, made the attack along with other aircraft, marking Japan's entrance into World War II. The single-engine, all-metal monoplanes put American battleships, cruisers, and other ships out of action.

**AILERONS.** Sections of the back edges of the wings that are hinged and can be raised or lowered. The ailerons are used for banking the aircraft to make turns.

**AIRBUS.** A wide-bodied airliner used for carrying large numbers of passengers short distances. The Airbus A 300 B made by Airbus Industries, an organization of several European airplane manufacturers, has 330 seats and is powered by two GE turbofan jets. The McDonnell Douglas DC-10 and Lockheed L-1011 TriStar are also airbuses.

**AIRCRAFT CARRIER.** A ship designed to carry aircraft and to serve as a floating surface for take-offs and landings. A typical carrier displaces about 70,000 tons (63,500 t), is more than 1,000 feet (305 m) long, carries about ninety aircraft, and sleeps about five thousand people. A flat upper deck, called the flight deck, serves as a take-off and landing field. The hangar deck is below the flight deck and is used for storing and servicing aircraft. Planes are moved from one deck to another by huge elevators.

Aircraft wait on the flight deck for launching. In modern aircraft-carrier operation, most aircraft take off under their own power. The carrier steams into the wind at take-off times to give added lift to the planes.

An angled section of the flight deck is used mostly for landing, which is also

**The U.S.S.**
*Enterprise*
**aircraft carrier**

called recovery. A series of steel cables which are strung across the angled deck catch the tail hook on the outside of the landing plane to stop it.

The first successful take-off and landing from an aircraft carrier took place in November 1910 from the cruiser U.S.S. *Birmingham*, which had an 83-foot (25.3-m) flat wooden platform erected on the foredeck. Eugene Ely, flying a Curtiss biplane, came in for a landing. Hooks on his landing gear caught stretched ropes and sandbags to help slow the plane to a stop.

In 1919 the U.S.S. *Jupiter*, a coal carrier, was converted to become the first aircraft carrier in the U.S. Navy. Dubbed the U.S.S. *Langley*, it went into service in 1922.

The first aircraft to operate from carriers were conventional biplanes at the end of World War I. By the late 1920s, specially designed fighter planes such as the Boeing F 4B-4 fighter were put into use. During World War II, aircraft carriers became the backbone of seaborne operations against enemy air power. Carrier planes were involved in every significant battle in the Pacific during World War II. The Battle of Midway, won by America, ended Japan's sweep across the Pacific.

**AIRFOIL.** A surface, such as a wing, aileron, or stabilizer, designed to aid in lifting or controlling an aircraft by making use of the air currents through which it moves.

**AIR FORCE.** The military unit of a nation charged with the responsibility of carrying out operations in the air. Each nation has its own way of organizing its air force. In some, the air force is a separate service, similar to the army and navy. In others, the air force is part of one of the other services.

The world's first air force, the Première Campagnie d'Aérostiers, was formed in France in 1794. On June 2 of that year, the French government sent up pilot Jean-Marie-Joseph Coutelle in a hydrogen balloon to report on Austrian and Dutch troop positions during the French Revolution. Coutelle ascended again on June 26 and, with the aid of observation and tactics directed from the air, the French emerged victorious. This marked the beginning of aerial warfare.

During the American Civil War, both the Federal and Confederate forces set up a balloon corps for observation. After the Civil War, most major armies in the world had balloon corps.

Air power developed rapidly during World War I. The Allies and Central Powers both used balloons to spot enemy submarines and direct artillery fire. At first, planes were used mostly for reconnaissance. As airplanes improved, they were used for combat ("dog fights"), bombing, and photographing enemy territory. Beginning in 1915, the Germans conducted raids in military aircraft.

By World War II air power had changed the nature of warfare. Planes were responsible for German victories in Poland, Norway, the Low Countries, and France. But the Allies achieved air superiority by means of increased engine power, advanced designs, better defensive armament, and the ability to fly higher, longer, at greater speeds, and with more maneuverability. Allied bombers, fighters, and transport planes were essential to victory.

Aircraft have been an important part of the military strategy of air forces since 1945. Rocket power, electronics, reconnaissance satellites, orbital bombers, and manned space vehicles will affect strategy in unforeseen ways in the future. *See also* U.S. AIR FORCE.

**AIRLINE.** A government or privately owned organization that operates aircraft to carry passengers and cargo in scheduled service.

**AIRLINER.** An aircraft built to carry passengers.

**AIRMAIL.** The system of carrying mail by airplane. The first airmail service took place in England and the United States in 1911. By 1918 U.S. Army pilots had begun regular airmail service for civilian mail. The first regular route was from New York City to Washington, D.C. In 1919 post office pilots began flying the dangerous New York-to-Chicago route over the Allegheny Mountains; it was called the "graveyard run." Open cockpits, lack of instruments, and bitter cold caused the deaths of thirty-one of the first forty pilots hired by the post office. Regular coast-to-coast service began in 1924. The following year Congress passed the Kelly Act, which allowed the government to use private airlines to carry the mail.

**AIR MEETS AND RACES.** The first great air meet was held at Reims, France, in August 1909 and lasted one week. Almost every flying pioneer took part. Henri Farman of France won the endurance prize by staying airborne for more than three hours. Glenn Curtiss was awarded a speed prize for averaging 47.65 mph (76.7 kph).

The first long-distance, cross-country airplane race was held in England on April 3, 1910. Englishman Claude Grahame-White left London on a Farman biplane powered by a 50 hp rotary engine. After flying for two hours, he landed at Rugby, a town 85 miles (136 km) from his starting point—a record-breaking flight.

**AIRPORT.** A place for the landing and taking off of aircraft. The runways of a modern airport are 9,000 to 14,000 feet (2,743 to 4,267 m) long. An airport has hangars to shelter, supply, and repair the planes. Included, too, are terminals for the passengers and freight, and offices for air traffic control, weather observation, and general administration.

**AIR POWER.** The use of aircraft in war.

**AIR RAIDS.** An attack by aircraft, especially the bombing of a particular area. During World War II massive air raids were directed at the hearts of several major European cities. Some involved more than a thousand planes. Toward the end of the Battle of Britain, Germans began to bomb London heavily. Later, raids were mounted against other British cities; one such raid destroyed the cathedral town of Conventry. As the war progressed, the Allies sent thousands of planes to raid the German cities of Cologne, Dusseldorf, and Dresden. They dropped thousands of tons of explosive and incendiary devices on the cities, turning them into raging infernos.

**AIRSHIP.** An aircraft that is lighter than air. Most airships get lift from the helium gas contained in the large bag in the hull or body of the airship. The power to move the aircraft through the air comes from engines and propellers suspended beneath the hull. All airships have a car or gondola inside or outside the hull in which to carry passengers and cargo. The crew controls the airship by means of devices similar to the rudder and elevator of an airplane.

There are two main types of airships: nonrigid and rigid. Nonrigid airships have a tight-fitting rubberized skin covering the hull. Their streamlined shape comes from the pressure of the gas within. Such nonrigid airships are called blimps. They are used mostly for patrol work. Rigid airships have an inside framework that supports the gas envelope. They are shaped by the framework, not from the pressure of the lifting gas envelope.

The first successful power-driven airship was built by Henri Giffard in 1852. In 1884 Charles Renard and A.C. Krebg achieved the first sustained and directed flight in their airship *La France.*

David Schwartz, an Austrian engineer, built the first rigid airship. But the most credit for advancing the airship goes to Count Ferdinand von Zeppelin of Germany. Zeppelin launched the first successful rigid airship on July 2, 1900, in Germany. It had a cigar-shaped metal frame covered with linen, contained 350,000 cubic feet (9,905 $m^3$) of hydrogen, and was propelled by two engines. Each engine drove two four-bladed propellers. Zeppelin had built twenty-six airships by the outbreak of World War I in 1914. The fastest could travel about 50 mph (80 kph).

During World War I the Germans used airships for bombing raids over England, as well as for reconnaissance. The British, too, built airships that were used mostly for military purposes. The British airships were not too successful, however, and were rarely used after 1919. The U.S. Navy built two rigid airships, the *Akron* and the *Macon,* in the early 1930s. Both were destroyed and lives were lost, ending America's activity with this type of airship. Construction of nonrigid blimps, however, continued from the beginning of World War II until the Navy ended its lighter-than-air aircraft program in 1961.

In Germany, the giant airship *Graf Zeppelin* was built in 1927. It was a huge ship, 787 feet (240 m) long and 100 feet (30 m) wide. In 1929 it traveled 20,000 miles (32,180 km) around the world. It could fly more than 70 mph (113 kph). The huge cabin could carry fifty passengers. Between 1933 and 1937, when it was taken out of service, it made dozens of Atlantic crossings.

The success of the *Graf Zeppelin* led to the building of the *Hindenburg* in 1936. The *Hindenburg* also had a rigid frame covered by fabric and was 812 feet (248 m) long, 135 feet (41 m) in diameter. The *Hindenburg* made fifty-four flights; thirty-six of them were transatlantic. While approaching Lakehurst, New Jersey, on May 6, 1937, the hydrogen-filled gas bag exploded, burning the airship and many of those aboard.

**AIRSICKNESS.** Feelings of dizziness and nausea due to the motion of the aircraft.

**AIR SURVEY.** Using a series of overlapping aerial photographs to map an area of land.

**ALBATROS D III CHASER.** This single-seat fighter biplane appeared at the end of 1916. It was built by Albatros Werke, one of Germany's most important aircraft companies. Powered with an engine of some 175 hp, this little "destroyer" inflicted great damage on Allied aircraft until airplanes that were still faster were developed. The speed of the *Albatros D III* was said to have been between 120 and 130 mph (193 and 209 kph). (Wingspan: upper, 30 feet [9 m]; lower, 29 feet [8.8 m].)

**ALCOCK, JOHN W.** (1892–1919). British winner, with Arthur Whitten Brown, of the London *Daily Mail* prize for a nonstop flight across the Atlantic Ocean. The two men made the flight in a remodelled Vickers *Vimy* two-engine bomber. They left from St. John's, Newfoundland, on June 14, 1919, and flew nearly sixteen and a half hours before landing in an Irish bog the next day. Alcock was killed in an air crash only six months later while flying in a Paris air show.

**ALTITUDE SICKNESS.** A condition similar to "mountain sickness," caused by a decrease in air pressure and the amount of oxygen. After just a short period one loses muscular control and sometimes consciousness. The condition may become chronic with repeated exposure to high altitudes. All modern aircraft have pressurized cabins to prevent altitude sickness.

**AMUNDSEN, ROALD** (1872–1928). A Norwegian explorer who made the first airship crossing of the North Pole on May 12, 1926. His dirigible, the *Norge*, was designed and commanded by the Italian airship expert, Umberto Nobile. Just two years later, Amundsen disappeared in the Arctic while searching by plane for Nobile, who was lost during an expedition to the North Pole. Nobile was found alive not long after.

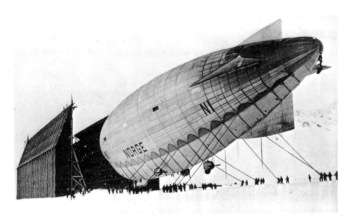

**The *Norge*, the first airship to cross the North Pole**

**ANDRÉE, SALOMON AUGUST** (1854–1897). A Swedish polar explorer who was the first to attempt to reach the North Pole by air. In 1897 Andrée and two companions set out in a balloon called the *Eagle*. They disappeared, and their bodies were found on White Island in 1930.

**ARNOLD, HENRY HARLEY ("HAP")** (1886–1950). An American general who was chief of the U.S. Army Air Forces from 1941 to 1946 . Due to Arnold's leadership in developing American air power, he is sometimes called "the father of the U.S. Air Force." He became general of the army in 1944 and later, in 1949, was made general of the air force—both "five star" ranks.

**AROUND-THE-WORLD FLIGHTS.** The first flight around the world was completed in 1924, after 175 days, by four U.S. Army pilots in two airplanes. The airplanes were the Douglas World Cruisers, *Chicago* and *New Orleans.* In August 1929 the second flight around the world was made from Germany in an airship called the *Graf Zeppelin.* The journey took a little more than three weeks, with stops at Tokyo, Los Angeles, and Lakehurst, New Jersey.

A successful flight around the world, taking only a little less than nine days, occurred in June and July 1931. The famous Lockheed Vega *Winnie Mae,* piloted by Wiley Post and navigator Harold Gatty, took off from Roosevelt Field, Long Island. Two years later, Wiley Post, flying alone, piloted the *Winnie Mae* around the world in less than eight days. He was the first person to fly solo around the world.

America's great pilot Amelia Earhart was lost in the Pacific with Fred Noonan, her navigator, while attempting an around-the-world flight in 1937. The following year Howard Hughes and his crew of four were able to circle the globe in less than four days. A U.S. Air Force crew flew the first nonstop around-the-world flight in 1949. Today flying around the world is commonplace and routine.

**AUTOGIRO.** An aircraft held in the air by a top rotor, like a helicopter, but with a front propeller, like an airplane. The rotor spins by itself as it passes through the air. The wingless autogiro also has an engine-driven nose propeller which pulls the plane forward. It cannot hover or fly sideways like a helicopter.

The autogiro, invented by the Spaniard Juan de la Cierva, was first flown in 1923. Later versions reached maximum speeds of 125 mph (201 kph). The autogiro has been almost completely replaced by the helicopter, although a few small autogiros are flown as recreational aircraft. *See also* CIERVA, JUAN DE LA.

**AVIATIK B1.** A two-seater German aircraft (1914) which was one of the first World War I planes to be used for reconnaissance. The plane carried two guns, a forward machine gun operated by the pilot and a rear gun manned by the observer.

**AVIATION.** The operation of aircraft heavier than air. Aviation includes piloting and air navigation, as well as all activities on which flying depends. Below are some of the most important milestones in lighter-than-air aircraft and in aviation history:

1200–1300   People first attempted to fly by attaching wings to their bodies.

1250   Roger Bacon proposed a gas-filled balloon.

1500   Leonardo da Vinci made scientific studies of flight; suggested a flying machine with wings; and devised ancestors of the helicopter and parachute.

1650   Italian Francesco de Lana published the first design for an airship.

1783   First flight in a hydrogen-filled balloon. J.A.C. Charles and M. Robert flew 25 miles (40 km). Also first hot-air balloon flight by Jean F. Pilâtre de Rozier and Marquis d'Arlandes in a Montgolfier balloon.

1785   First crossing of the English Channel by air. John Jeffries and Jean-Pierre Blanchard flew in a hydrogen balloon from England to France.

1804   First successful model glider, built by Sir George Cayley.

1843   William S. Henson patented a design for a steam-driven airplane that foreshadowed the modern monoplane.

1848   John Stringfellow made and flew a model airplane that is said to be the first power-driven machine to fly.

1866   F.H. Wenham contributed valuable study on the laws of flight. Five years later Wenham designed the first wind-tunnel experiments.

1890   Clément Ader, French engineer, achieved a distance of about 150 feet (46 m) in a power-driven monoplane.

1894   The English inventor Sir Hiram S. Maxim built a plane, operated by steam engines, which lifted equipment and a crew of three into the air.

1891–1896   German inventor Otto Lilienthal made the first successful glider flights which are said to have inspired the Wright brothers.

1903   The first successful flight in man-carrying powered airplane by the Wright brothers at Kitty Hawk, North Carolina, on December 17.

1909   The first successful airplane crossing of the English Channel by Louis Blériot of France. The trip took thirty-seven minutes.

1912   Glenn Curtiss flew the first successful flying boat or seaplane.

1918    The first regular air mail delivery in the world was started by U.S. Army pilots on May 15. Air mail was taken over by the Post Office department on August 12.

1919    First nonstop airplane flight across the Atlantic was undertaken by British fliers John Alcock and A.W. Brown on June 14. The 1,936-mile (3,115-km) trip took 15 hours, 57 minutes.

1924    The first round-the-world flight took place from April 5 to September 28. Two U.S. Army biplanes flew 26,345 miles (42,389 km) in 175 days.

1926    The first flight over the North Pole in an airplane was made on May 9 by Richard E. Byrd and Floyd Bennett.

         The first airship flight over the North Pole took place from May 11 through May 14, with explorer Roald Amundsen, Umberto Nobile, and Lincoln Ellsworth on board.

1927    The first nonstop solo flight across the Atlantic in an airplane was flown by Charles A. Lindbergh on May 20 and 21. He flew 3,610 miles (5,806 km) in 33 hours, 30 minutes.

1929    The first around-the-world flight by an airship was made by the *Graf Zeppelin* in 21 days, 8 hours, from August 8 to 29.

1932    The first transatlantic solo flight by a woman was made by Amelia Earhart, who flew from Canada to Ireland on May 20 and 21 in 15 hours, 18 minutes.

1933    The first solo round-the-world airplane flight, by Wiley Post, took place from July 15 to 22, lasting 7 days, 18 hours, 49 minutes.

1939    The first jet-powered airplane was built by the Heinkel Company in Germany.

1940    The first successful flight of a single rotor helicopter took place on May 21, at Stratford, Connecticut, by Igor Sikorsky.

1947    The first flight faster than the speed of sound was made by U.S. Air Force Capt. Charles Yeager in a rocket-powered Bell X-1.

1955    Turboprop airliners were put into service by the major United States airlines.

1959     Jet airliners began regularly scheduled flights in the United States on January 25.

1961     The first man to fly in outer space was Yuri A. Gagarin of Russia on April 12. On May 5, Alan B. Shepard, Jr. became the first American to make a space flight.

1962     On February 20, astronaut John H. Glenn, Jr., completed three orbits around the earth in a space flight that lasted nearly five hours.

1969     On July 20, Apollo 11 landed on the moon, and Neil Armstrong became the first person to walk on the moon's surface.

1981     The first space shuttle, *Columbia,* was launched on April 12 and returned to earth fifty-four hours later.

### AVIATION RECORDS.

**Fastest Speed, Jet Aircraft:**
2,193.16 mph (3,528.79 kph)
Capt. Eldon W. Joersz, USAF
July 1976
Lockheed SR-71

**Longest Distance, Jet Aircraft:**
12,532.28 miles (20,164.44 km)
Maj. Clyde P. Evely, USAF
January 1962
Boeing B 52-H

**Highest Altitude, Jet Aircraft:**
23.39 miles (37.64 km)
Alexander Fedetov (USSR)
August 1977
E-226 M

**Highest Altitude, Rocket Aircraft:**
59.6 miles (95.9 km)
Maj. Robert M. White, USAF
July 1962
North American X-15-1

**Longest Distance, Sailplane:**
907.7 miles (1,460.5 km)
Hans Werner Grosse (Germany)
April 1972
ASK 12 Sailplane

**Highest Altitude, Sailplane:**
8.76 miles (14 km)
Paul F. Bikle (U.S.)
February 1961
Schweizer SCG 123 E. Sailplane

**Man-Powered Aircraft Flight:**
Duration—2 hours, 49 minutes
Distance—22.26 miles (35.8 km)
Bryan Allen (U.S.)
June 1979
*Gossamer Albatross*

**Balloon Flight:**
Duration—137 hours, 6 minutes
Distance—3,107.61 miles (5,000 km)
Ben L. Abruzzo, Maxie L. Anderson, Larry M. Newman (U.S.)
August 1978

**AVRO LANCASTER.** A British bomber (1942) flown by the Royal Air Force (RAF) during World War II. The Mark III model had a top speed of 270 mph (434 kph) and a ceiling of 21,500 feet (6,550 m). Although it was built to carry 8,000 pounds (3,629 kg) of bombs, some later versions were able to carry a 22,000-pound (9,979-kg) bomb. It was armed with three .303 machine guns.

The Lancaster is famous for its performance in air raids on the Moehne and Eder dams in Germany during World War II. Hydroelectric power from these dams was vital to German industry, and they were very well protected. The Lancasters, though, were able to penetrate the defenses and destroy the dams, using special bombs. (Wingspan, 102 feet [31 m]; length, 69 feet 6 inches [21 m].)

**AWACS.** *See* BOEING E-3A AWACS.

**B17.** *See* BOEING B-17.
**B-36.** *See* CONVAIR B-36.
**B-58.** *See* CONVAIR B-58 HUSTLER.

**BAC-AÉROSPATIALE CONCORDE.** The original supersonic transport (SST) (*see* SST) jet airliner (1969) to be put into regular commercial service. The plane was jointly developed and built by the British Aircraft Corporation and Aérospatiale of France. Using four Rolls-Royce turbojets, the Concorde has a cruising speed of 1,350 mph (2,170 kph) and a range of 4,000 miles (6,440 km). The ceiling for the Concorde is 11 miles (18 km). It can carry a maximum of 144 passengers.

The nose of the Concorde is lowered at take-off and landing to improve the pilot's range of vision. The Concorde lifts off the ground at a speed of about 200 mph (322 kph). Around 100 miles (160 km) from land the plane accelerates to supersonic speeds. A sonic boom is produced when the aircraft begins to fly faster than the speed of sound.

The wings of the Concorde are shaped like a triangle. The wing shape permits the pilot to land the plane at the relatively low speed of 180 mph (290 kph).

**A BAC-
Aérospatiale
Concorde**

The chief advantage of the Concorde, of course, is its great speed. Travel time between New York and London is three and a half hours as compared to seven hours on a subsonic plane. Los Angeles to Honolulu, a trip that usually takes five hours, is cut in half on the Concorde. (Wingspan, 84 feet [26 m]; length, 202 feet [62 m].)

**BALLOON.** A large bag, or envelope, filled with a gas that is lighter than air, which provides the lift. Most modern balloons are made of nylon. They are filled with hot air, which is lighter than the surrounding air. A basket, which is attached to the balloon, holds the pilot and crew.

The pilot produces the hot air by turning on a burner beneath an opening in the balloon, heating the air inside. To descend, the pilot simply allows the air inside the balloon to cool.

The first hot air balloon was designed in 1783 by the brothers Joseph and Jacques Étienne Montgolfier, who were papermakers in France. A bonfire was used to heat the air in the balloon so that it could rise. The first manned balloon flight took place on November 21, 1783, and lasted twenty-five minutes.

The first crossing of the English Channel by balloon was made in 1785. Balloons were used to carry messages in and out of Paris during the war of 1870. Armies observed enemy lines from balloons in World War I, and used unmanned, high-flying balloons to protect cities and military camps from attack planes and dive bombers during World War II.

In recent years, using balloons for sport and recreation has become popular. In 1978 three Americans set the record for duration and distance in their flight across the Atlantic Ocean.

Unmanned balloons that carry various measuring instruments are a valuable and important tool of modern weather forecasting. *See also* AVIATION RECORDS.

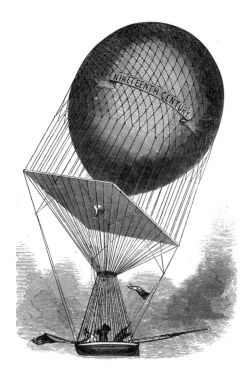

**A nineteenth-century balloon**

**BARNSTORMERS.** Pilots who gave exhibitions of stunt flying or racing. After World War I many flyers were out of work. They traveled from town to town performing stunts in war-surplus DH 4's and Curtiss *Jenny* training planes before large crowds. The influence of barnstorming on the nation was significant. Not only did it impress observers with the marvels of flying, but it kept aviation alive until the start of commercial flights.

**BEACHEY, LINCOLN** (1887–1915). The stunt flyer whom Orville Wright called "the greatest aviator of all." Beachey began his career in aviation as a balloonist. After he learned to fly a plane he became known as an exhibition pilot. Among his many tricks was lifting a handkerchief off the airfield with the wing tip of his plane. Beachey "looped the loop" more than a thousand times and also demonstrated flying under bridges. A special stunt was the "death dive" in which Beachey would plunge nearly vertically and land in a prearranged spot. On March 14, 1915, at an exhibition in San Francisco, the wings of Beachey's plane folded while in a dive and the pilot fell to his death.

**BEECHCRAFT.** A line of general aviation planes made by the Beech Aircraft Corporation. Beechcraft are mostly light aircraft that are bought and used by businesses for executive travel. One popular aircraft, the *Beech Bonanza,* is easily recognized by its distinctive V-shaped tail surface.

**BELL 47.** A helicopter (1945) that was manufactured in the United States for twenty-eight years and is still being built in other countries. The Bell 47 is only a little more than 31 feet (10 m) long. Originally a three-seater, later models have four or five seats. The aircraft is used for many purposes, including traffic control, sightseeing, military observation, and light cargo hauling.

**BELL X-1.** The first rocket-propelled research aircraft. Built in 1945, this single-seat plane was first designed for jet propulsion, but was modified to be rocket-powered. The X-1, which looked like a bullet with wings, burned alcohol and liquid oxygen for a thrust of 6,000 pounds (2,722 kg).

**Test pilot Chalmers Goodlin and the Bell X-1**

On October 14, 1947, the X-1 made history by being the first plane to fly faster than the speed of sound. Piloted by U.S. Air Force Capt. Charles E. Yeager, the plane attained a speed of 760 mph (1,223 kph). Since the X-1 could fly for only two and a half minutes, it was carried aloft by another plane and launched in the air. Not long after its first flight, Yeager flew the X-1 at a record 956 mph (1,538 kph). The plane has a maximum speed of 1,700 mph (2,735 kph). (Wingspan, 28 feet [8.5 m]; length, 31 ft [9 m]).

**BENDIX TROPHY.** A highly prized award presented for highest speed in an airplane, awarded from 1931 to 1939. The Bendix Transcontinental Air Race was founded by Vincent Bendix (1882–1945), an American inventor. He donated the trophy to anyone who won the cross-country competition race that was open to all flying planes of any size and with any type of engine. James H. Doolittle was awarded the Bendix Trophy after he won the first race in 1931. Doolittle completed a California-to-Ohio trip in 11 hours, 16 minutes. For the rest of the decade, speed record after record was broken as new and better planes and engines were developed.

**BENNETT, FLOYD** (1890–1928). An American aviator who piloted the first airplane to reach the North Pole. Together with Richard E. Byrd, Bennett made a non-stop flight from Spitsbergen (now Svalbard), Norway, to the North Pole and back in a three-engine Fokker aircraft on May 9, 1926. The 1,545-mile (2,486-km) trip took 15 hours and 30 minutes. The trip was particularly dangerous because there were no landmarks to guide the fliers. Bennett met an untimely death from pneumonia after he left his sickbed to rescue the stranded crew of the Junkers *Bremen* at Greely Island.

**BENNETT CUP.** A trophy for balloon and airplane races established by American newspaper owner James Gordon Bennett, Jr. (1841–1918).

**BENOIST FLYING BOAT.** An aircraft used as early as January 1, 1914, to carry passengers from St. Petersburg to Tampa, Florida, on the first scheduled airline, the Airboat Line. The flying boat used by the line carried only one passenger at ten dollars per round trip. It took twenty minutes to cover 22 miles (35 km). Although the Airboat Line failed, it did carry twelve hundred passengers in only three months. The schedule read: ''Trips covering any distance over all water routes, and from the water's surface to several thousand feet high AT PASSENGER'S REQUEST.''

**BERLIN AIRLIFT.** The use of aircraft in 1948 and 1949 to carry food and supplies to the German city of West Berlin. At the end of World War II in 1945, West Berlin lay inside the Russian zone of occupied Germany. In the summer of 1948, the Russians tried to force the British, American, and French troops from the city by cutting off supply routes into West Berlin. To keep West Berlin supplied, the Allies flew cargo planes into the city at three-minute intervals day and night. In May 1949, the Russians backed off and allowed the Allies to use overland routes again. The airlift had broken the blockade.

**BERNOULLI, DANIEL** (1700–1782). Mathematician and physicist who advanced the kinetic theory of gases and fluids. Bernoulli stated the principle, known as Bernoulli's Law, that fast-moving air has a lower pressure than slower-moving air. The air passing over the curved top of an aircraft wing is moving faster than the air passing beneath the flat bottom of the wing. The lower pressure above pulls the plane up and provides the lift necessary for flight.

**BIPLANE.** An aircraft with two sets of wings, one above the other.

**BIRD OF PARADISE.** *See* FOKKER BIRD OF PARADISE.

**BLANCHARD, JEAN-PIERRE** (1753–1809). A French balloonist who was an aviation pioneer. In 1785, with Dr. John Jeffries of Boston, Massachusetts, Blanchard made the first crossing by air of the English Channel. He is said to have made more than sixty balloon ascents, a record for about fifty years.

**BLÉRIOT, LOUIS** (1872–1936). A French aviator and inventor who was the first to cross the English Channel on July 25, 1909, in a monoplane. For his effort, Blériot won the London *Daily Mail* prize of £1,000. After the Channel crossing the Blériot monoplane became very popular, and Blériot became a well-known manufacturer of monoplanes. Generally he is credited with inventing and building the prototype of the monoplane which has not changed much since then. He suffered many accidents and was involved in about fifty crashes, but he kept constructing and flying planes until his death.

**BLÉRIOT XI.** A monoplane built in 1909 that is one of the most famous of the early airplanes. The single-seat plane was designed and flown by Louis Blériot when he made the first crossing of the English Channel. The flight, a distance of about 24 miles (38 km), began at 4:41 A.M. and ended at 5:17 A.M. The average speed was 36 mph (58 kph). (Wingspan, 25 feet 7 inches [7.7 m]; length, 26 feet 3 inches [8 m].) *See also* BLÉRIOT, LOUIS.

**BLIMP.** A nonrigid lighter-than-air aircraft that is basically a sealed, shaped balloon filled with gas. The best known example is the Goodyear blimp, used for advertising and as a platform for television cameras over major sporting events. The name is made up of the letter ''B'' from balloon, and ''limp,'' which describes the balloon before being inflated. *See also* AIRSHIP, BALLOON, and DIRIGIBLE.

**BLITZKRIEG.** A term that describes Germany's fast-moving attack in the early part of World War II by air forces, ground troups, and armored vehicles on various nations in Europe. Blitzkrieg literally means ''lightning war.'' Once the German air force, the Luftwaffe, gained control of the skies over Poland, they conquered the nation. In short order, German air power helped them occupy Norway, Denmark, the Netherlands, Luxembourg, Belgium, and France. The Germans used bombers such as the Heinkel He 111, Junkers Ju 88, and Dornier Do 17 to attack ground targets while the Messerschmidt Bf 109 and Bf 110 acted as fighters and attack planes.

**BOEING COMPANY.** One of the world's largest and most successful designers and manufacturers of aircraft. The company was founded by engineer William Boeing (1881–1956) in 1916. During World War I the firm built planes for the U.S. Navy. In March 1919 Boeing started an airmail line between Victoria, Canada, and Seattle, Washington, which also served as passenger transportation because the planes could carry four people. Boeing introduced air hostesses in 1930. The first stewardesses were nurses.

**BOEING B-17 FLYING FORTRESS.** A propeller bomber (1935) that was the first of the famous World War II series of flying fortresses and probably the best known of all American military aircraft. With four Wright engines putting out 930 hp, it could achieve a top speed of 256 mph (412 kph), a ceiling of 30,600 feet (9,327 m), and a range of 3,320 miles (5,342 km). A bomb load of 10,500 pounds (4,763 kg) could be carried. The craft was armed with five machine guns, either .30 or .50 calibre. A crew of six was required.

By 1942 the plane had evolved into the B-17F, with a speed of 299 mph

(481 kph), a ceiling of 37,500 feet (11,430 m), and a range of 2,880 miles (4,634 km). It was armed with eleven .50 calibre machine guns.

In September 1943 the B-17G, which had an added machine gun turret, was ready for production. Altogether, 8,680 B-17Gs were built, the largest number of the B-17 series. Its four Wright supercharged engines delivered 1,200 hp for a top speed of 287 mph (462 kph), a ceiling of 35,600 feet (10,850 m), and a range of 3,400 miles (5,470 km). By the time production of Flying Fortresses ended in 1945 a total of 12,731 had been made. (Wingspan, 103 feet 9 inches [32 m]; length, 74 feet 4 inches [23 m].)

**A Boeing B-17
Flying Fortress**

**BOEING B-29 SUPERFORTRESS.** A propeller bomber (1942) with four Wright 2,200 hp engines to power its propellers and a top speed of 267 mph (430 kph), the B-29 was indeed an exceptional plane. Up to 20,000 pounds (9,072 kg) of bombs could be carried over a range of 3,250 miles (5,229 km), with a ceiling of 21,850 feet (6,660 m). In addition to machine guns, the Super-fortress was equipped with a 20 mm cannon. Nearly four thousand aircraft were built before production ended in 1945. The B-29 *Enola Gay* dropped the atomic bomb on Hiroshima, Japan, on August 6, 1945. Another B-29, *Bock's Car,* dropped the bomb that destroyed Nagasaki. (Wingspan, 141 feet 3 inches [43 m]; length, 99 feet [30 m].)

**BOEING B-52 STRATOFORTRESS.** A jet bomber (1952) that was constructed as a replacement for the B-36s. The B-52 is probably the last of the giant bombers. It has swept-back wings and eight Pratt & Whitney jet engines that each provide 9,700 pounds (4,400 kg) of thrust. Later planes in the series have new engines, each one with 17,000 pounds (7,711 kg) of thrust. While much of the information on the B-52s is classified, it is believed that they have a top speed of 650 mph (1,046 kph) and a ceiling of more than 60,000 feet (18,288 m). The range is more than 10,000 miles (16,090 km) because the wing itself is a gigantic fuel tank. The B-52 can carry up to 65,000 pounds (29,484 kg) of bombs.

The primary offensive weapons of the B-52s are missiles. The six-person crew of the B-52 is armed with a cannon and machine guns. The B-52 is also used to carry aloft the X-15 experimental rocket aircraft for in-flight launching. Production ended in 1962 after 744 B-52s had been made. (Wingspan, 185 feet [56 m]; length, 157 feet 7 inches [48 m].) *See also* NORTH AMERICAN X-15.

**BOEING E-3A AWACS (Airborne Warning and Control System).** AWACS, as this aircraft is usually called, provides radar observation over vast distances. The aircraft itself is adapted from a 707 airliner. *See also* BOEING 707.

**BOEING 307 STRATOLINER.** A propeller airliner (1938), this was the first plane with a pressurized cabin. With this equipment, the Stratoliner was able to fly above bad weather without the need for passengers to wear oxygen masks. The Stratoliner carried thirty-three passengers. Using the wing and tail design of the B-17 Flying Fortress and with four 1,100 hp engines driving the four propellers, the Stratoliner had a top speed of 246 mph (396 kph) and a range of 2,390 miles (3,850 km). During World War II a number of Stratoliners were adapted for military transport and identified as C-75s. (Wingspan, 107 feet 3 inches [33 m]; length, 74 feet 4 inches [23 m].)

**BOEING 707.** A jet airliner (1957) that was the first, and one of the most successful, passenger-carrying jets. Starting work in 1952, the Boeing Company spent about $20 million to develop the 707. It was the workhorse of the 1960s, used to fly both to Europe and from coast to coast. The 707 introduced cheap, mass air travel to the world. It has four Pratt & Whitney engines slung under the wings. Each one produces 18,000 pounds (8,165 kg) of thrust, allowing it to cruise at 550 mph (885 kph) for a 4,300-mile (7,000-km) range. The 707 can carry as many as 219 passengers. About a thousand 707s were built through the late 1970s. (Wingspan, 145 feet 9 inches [44 m]; length, 152 feet 11 inches [47 m].)

**The Boeing 707 takes off on its first test flight.**

**BOEING 747.** The world's largest civilian aircraft and the first jumbo jet, the 747 was introduced in 1969. It can easily be identified by the bulge of the double deck in the front part of the fuselage. With a cabin 20 feet (6 m) wide and 186 feet (57 m) long, the 747 can carry about five hundred passengers. For most of its length, which is divided into five separate sections, there is room for ten seats across.

The 747's range is 5,100 miles (8,206 km). It has four Pratt & Whitney turbofan jets under the wings, each jet putting out 46,950 pounds (21,296 kg) of thrust. The three- or four-person crew can cruise along at 625 mph (1,007 kph) at an altitude of 30,000 feet (9,000 m). (Wingspan, 195 feet 8 inches [60 m]; length, 231 feet 4 inches [71 m].)

**BOEING VERTOL CH-47 CHINOOK.** The standard medium-lift attack helicopter (1962) used by the U.S. Army during the Vietnam War. Its twin rotors give the Chinook the ability to carry or lift heavy loads. The craft can carry 13,450 pounds (6,000 kg) of cargo, or up to forty-four fully equipped troops. One of the main uses of the Chinook during the Vietnam War was to pick up downed American aircraft and bring them back to base for repairs. Since the bulky, wrecked craft could not fit inside the fuselage, they were usually hung beneath the Chinook for the trip. The helicopter is 99 feet (31 m) long and has a top speed of 201 mph (323 kph).

**BOELCKE, OSWALD** (1891–1916). One of Germany's first and most outstanding aces. Boelcke was said to be modest, brave, and a natural leader. He was given the responsibility of developing fighter squadrons during World War I. Boelcke flew the Albatros D I. While in combat in 1916, Boelcke's fighter was brushed by one of his own squadron's planes. The impact sent Boelcke's plane out of control and he died in the crash.

**BOMBER.** An aircraft built for dropping bombs on enemy targets. The very first bombers were nothing more than planes with open cockpits, from which the pilots tossed small, hand-held bombs. Modern bombers carry explosive bombs, nuclear bombs, and missiles, either in the fuselage or beneath the wings. Most bombers are identified by the letter B followed by a number, such as the B-52.

**BONG, RICHARD IRA** (1920–1945). The highest scoring American ace and top American fighter pilot of World War II. By war's end, Bong had shot down forty enemy aircraft. He taught student pilots how to fight the Japanese. Bong was killed while testing a new jet plane just before the end of the war.

**BORELLI, GIOVANNI ALFONSO** (1608–1679). An Italian physicist and astronomer who set forth a theory of the mechanics of flight in *De Moto Animalium* (Concerning Animal Motion). He wrote that humans simply did not have the muscle power to fly like birds. Therefore, he said he had "no faith in any invention designed to lift man from the earth."

**BRITAIN, BATTLE OF.** The combat between the air forces of Germany and Britain for control of the skies over England and the English Channel that began in the summer of 1940. Germany bombed British ships and ports and aimed to destroy all Royal Air Force airfields and installations. With the use of radar, the British were able to spot approaching enemy planes and send out RAF Spitfire and Hurricane fighters to engage them in battle. By breaking the German code, they learned where bombers intended to strike. And ground-to-air radio communications allowed officers to direct planes to change direction if necessary.

In August 1940 the German Luftwaffe began to bomb the cities of Britain. Large parts of London were destroyed. The move only stiffened British resistance. In September Germany postponed and then abandoned plans to invade England, largely because the RAF was winning the Battle of Britain and gaining control of the skies over England.

**BYRD, RICHARD EVELYN** (1888–1957). An American rear admiral, aviator, and explorer who was the first person to fly over both North and South poles. On May 9, 1926, Byrd and Floyd Bennett flew from Spitsbergen (now Svalbard), Norway, to the North Pole and back. Byrd's first Antarctic expedition, from 1928 to 1930, established a base, Little America, at the Bay of Whales. The second Byrd expedition to the Antarctic, from 1933 to 1935, gathered much scientific information about the region.

World War II ended exploration of the Antarctic and Byrd served in the Department of the Navy. In 1947 and 1956 Byrd made his second and third flights over the South Pole. He continued to work on plans for Antarctic exploration until his death.

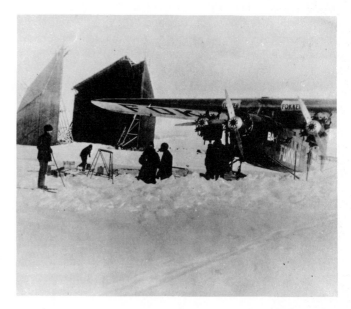

**Richard Byrd and his Fokker aircraft at the South Pole**

**CANTILEVER WING.** A type of construction in which no external bracing is used to support the wings. The invention was patented by Hugo Junkers.

**CAPRONI BOMBERS.** A series of multi-engine bombers, introduced by the wealthy Italian builder, Count Gianni Caproni (1886–1957). The CA 4s were used during World War I on long missions over the Alps and Balkan mountains against the forces of the empire of Austria-Hungary. They were equipped with three engines, and some carried bomb loads of up to 3,200 pounds (1,450 kg). Most were armed with machine guns. Toward the end of the war, triple-engine CA 5 biplanes were put into service.

**CAYLEY, SIR GEORGE** (1773–1857). A pioneer in the science of aeronautics whose studies laid the groundwork for successful flight. As a young person Cayley investigated the principles of bird flight. He discarded the popular idea at the time of imitating bird flight by flapping wings. In 1804 he built the first model glider. It was 5 feet (1.5 m) long and closely resembled today's airplane. Many accept this glider as the first airplane and call Cayley "the father of aerial navigation." From studies on the glider, Cayley derived much useful information. Toward the end of his life, after thirty years of theoretical work, Cayley built a glider large enough to carry a person, and saw it flown for a short distance by his coachman.

**CEILING.** The maximum altitude an aircraft can reach. Also, the maximum height that can be seen from earth; usually equal to the distance of the lowest clouds.

**CESSNA.** A line of light aircraft founded in 1927 by the pioneer American aviator Clyde V. Cessna. Cessna had been building airplanes since 1911. The company he began is one of the world's largest makers of craft for general aviation. To date, it has already manufactured more than 200,000 planes. Most of the craft are used for business or agriculture. The most popular models are the 172 Skyhawk and 150.

**A Cessna 407**

**CHANCE VOUGHT F-4U CORSAIR.** A propeller fighter plane first flown in 1940, the Corsair is characterized by its distinctive W-shaped wing. The plane was co-designed by Igor Sikorsky (1889–1972), the famous helicopter manufacturer, and was one of the most successful fighters in service during World War II. The craft was used mostly in the Pacific.

**CHANCE VOUGHT F-8 CRUSADER.** The first U.S. carrier-borne supersonic aircraft. It entered service in 1957. The plane's two-position wing allows it to perform well in supersonic flight and during low-speed approaches for deck landings. Modified versions of this plane were used in photo reconnaissance. They helped reveal the presence of Soviet missile sites in Cuba in the early 1960s. (Wingspan, 35 feet 8 inches [11 m]; length, 54 feet 3 inches [17 m].)

**CIERVA, JUAN DE LA** (1895–1936). A Spanish engineer who developed the autogiro and laid the foundation for today's helicopters. Cierva chose the name autogiro for his invention, first flown on January 9, 1923, which could take off and land within very confined spaces at slow speeds. It became the trade name of the Cierva Autogiro Company.

**CLIMB INDICATOR.** An instrument that shows the rate of ascent or descent of an aircraft.

**COCKPIT.** The control center of an aircraft with seats for the pilot, co-pilot, and a flight engineer. Within easy reach or sight of these crew members are the more than two hundred controls and instruments.

**The cockpit of a Boeing 747**

**COCKPIT VOICE RECORD (CVR).** A recording device that is found on all airliners and is common on combat aircraft. If something goes wrong and the aircraft crashes, the CVR provides vital information for investigators. The crash recorder is played back on a regular basis to check piloting standards and to aid in maintenance of the aircraft.

**CONCORDE.** *See* BAC-AÉROSPATIALE CONCORDE.

**CONSOLIDATED B-24 LIBERATOR.** A propeller bomber that was first introduced in 1939. More Liberators were built, nearly twenty thousand, than any other military aircraft during World War II. Although it had distinctive twin fins, the B-24 was similar to the B-17 Flying Fortress. The first B-24s had four propellers driven by Pratt & Whitney engines and could fly at nearly 300 mph (480 kph). The aircraft were armed with ten .50 machine guns, and could carry up to 8,800 pounds (4,000 kg) of bombs. (Wingspan, 110 feet [33.53 m]; length, 67 feet 2 inches [20.47 m].)

**CONVAIR AIRCRAFT.** An American aircraft manufacturer founded in 1923 by Maj. Reuben H. Fleet as Consolidated Aircraft. The Consolidated Husky was the principal military training plane between the wars. During World War II, the company produced thirty-three thousand planes, more than any other manufacturer in the world. In 1953 Convair became part of the General Dynamics Corporation.

**CONVAIR B-36.** A propeller jet bomber (1946) that was the largest aircraft of its time. The B-36D had six propellers and four jet engines, and required a crew of twenty-two. Because of its long, thin fuselage, the B-36 was nicknamed "The Flying Cigar." It was originally designed to make bombing runs from the United States to Europe. The B-36 had a top speed of 439 mph (706 kph) and could remain in the air for twenty-four hours or longer with in-flight refueling. A joke among B-36 crews was that the planes should have been built with a calendar! A total of 325 B-36s was built in a series that ended with the B-36Hs. The last B-36 was retired in 1958. (Wingspan, 230 feet [70 m]; length, 163 feet [50 m].)

**CONVAIR B-58 HUSTLER.** The first supersonic jet bomber (1956), the Convair B-58 flew at Mach 2, twice the speed of sound. The aircraft was unique in a few ways. The wing was delta-shaped, that is, in the shape of a large triangle. The needle-pointed fuselage was so narrow that there was no room for the usual bomb bay. Therefore, a special pod was attached below to carry the weapons, such as bombs or missiles.

**A Convair
B-58 Hustler**

The plane was covered by two sheets of aluminum with air space in between to withstand the intense heat built up by the supersonic speeds. With four General Electric jet engines producing 16,000 pounds (7,258 kg) of thrust each, the B-58 flew at a speed of 1,385 mph (2,228 kph) with a ceiling of 60,000 feet (18,288 m). The three crewmen had a 20 mm cannon in the rear for protection. Because of its delta wing, the Hustler needed to be moving at the high speed of 230 mph (370 kph) at takeoff. This bomber was taken out of service in 1970. (Wingspan, 56 feet 10 inches [17 m]; length, 96 feet 9 inches [30 m].)

**CONVAIR F-102 DELTA DAGGER.** The first delta-winged jet fighter plane (1953) used by the U.S. Air Force. A single Pratt & Whitney jet with a thrust of 17,200 pounds (7,802 kg) gave the Delta Dagger a top speed of 825 mph (1,327 kph). The armament consisted of six air-to-air missiles. The last Delta Dagger left service in 1975. (Wingspan, 38 feet 1 inch [12 m]; length, 68 feet 4 inches [20 m].)

**CONVERTIPLANE (CVT).** A type of experimental aircraft that is able to take off and land vertically and to fly horizontally. Convertiplanes can operate like helicopters and hover in the air using rotors and fans, or travel forward like conventional aircraft.

An early convertiplane was the McDonnell XV-1 equipped with a jet-powered rotor for vertical flight and a propeller engine for forward flight. The first vertical flight of the XV-1 took place in April 1955.

A later development was the Bell XV-3, first flown in August 1955. The XV-3 had one propulsion system for both horizontal and vertical flight. Lift was provided by wing-tip mounted rotors that could then be tilted for level flight. CVTs are also called VTOLs (vertical takeoff and landing) and STOLs (short takeoff and landing).

**CORNU HELICOPTER.** A twin-rotor helicopter (1907) in which the Frenchman, Paul Cornu, is widely considered to have been first to achieve flight with a rotary-winged aircraft. On November 13, 1907, the helicopter lifted Cornu about 1 foot (0.3 m) from the ground. The test lasted about twenty seconds. Some claim that Louis Breguet and Professor Richet made the first manned helicopter ascent on September 29, 1907. This slightly earlier flight, however, was stabilized by four men holding a pole under each rotor.

**CURTISS, GLENN HAMMOND** (1878–1930). An important developer and manufacturer of aircraft during World War I. In 1908 Curtiss helped design an airplane called the *June Bug.* It had a box tail and was controlled by ailerons, which were hinged flaps on the wings. The Wright brothers sued and won a court case against Curtiss, charging that the ailerons violated their patent on a method of controlling flight that used twisting wings.

Curtiss built the first planes for the U.S. Navy in 1911 after convincing them to build a wooden platform on the deck of the cruiser *Birmingham* for takeoffs and landings. From this came the modern aircraft carriers. The Curtiss P-40 Kittyhawk and Tomahawk were attack planes used during World War II.

**CURTISS HAWK.** A series of fighter aircraft. The first Hawk, a single-seat biplane, was the chief U.S. Army fighter from 1925 to 1933. (Wingspan, 32 feet [10 m]; length, 22 feet 6 inches [7 m].) The name Hawk was also used for the P-36 monoplane fighter which was Curtiss' first all-metal aircraft. Although it was obsolete by 1941, it was still operational at the time of the Japanese attack on Pearl Harbor. (Wingspan, 37 feet 4 inches [11 m]; length, 28 feet 6 inches [9 m].)

**CURTISS HELLDIVER.** A series of Navy and Marine Corps dive-bombers developed in the years between the wars. The first Helldivers were biplanes. The Curtiss SB2C Helldiver, first flown in 1940, served as the standard U.S. Navy dive-bomber from 1943 to 1946. A total of 7,194 Helldivers were built; 900 were for Army Air Forces' use.

**D VII.** *See* FOKKER D VII.

**DC-3.** *See* DOUGLAS DC-3.

**DAIMLER-BENZ.** A well-known manufacturer of aircraft engines. The parent firm, Daimler, was founded by Gottlieb Daimler (1834–1900), a German engineer, and Karl Benz (1844–1929), who developed the internal combustion engine for automobiles and produced engines for powered flight. Before World War I, all gasoline engines used by Count Zeppelin's airships were made by Daimler or Benz. During the war years, both Daimler and Benz developed a number of six-cylinder water-cooled engines. These engines were used in the Fokker D VII, in Albatros scouts, and in many other aircraft.

The Daimler and Benz companies merged in 1926 to produce airship diesel engines and water-cooled gasoline engines which were later used to power the German *Luftwaffe*'s wartime aircraft.

**DASSAULT-BREGUET.** France's largest privately owned aircraft manufacturer. The most successful planes of Dassault are the Mirage fighter planes, which were put into production in 1959. In December 1971 Dassault merged with Société Louis Breguet, France's oldest aircraft manufacturer, to form Dassault-Breguet.

**DASSAULT MIRAGE.** A series of French-made jet fighter planes introduced in 1955 that have been made available to a number of air forces, including France's, South Africa's, Pakistan's, and Israel's. Different planes in the series were built with traditional wings, delta wings, and swing wings. One of the most advanced models is the Mirage 2000. This single-seater aircraft has a top speed of more than Mach 2.3. (Wingspan, 30 feet [9 m]; length, 48 feet [15 m].)

**DEAD STICK LANDING.** A landing of an airplane without engine power.

**DE HAVILLAND AIRCRAFT COMPANY.** A major British manufacturer of aircraft that was formed in 1920 by Geoffrey de Havilland (1882–1965). Before and during World War I, De Havilland worked for other companies building the DH I pusher plane and the DH 4 single-engine bomber. After the war, the firm produced its most successful civil plane, the DH 18, which carried passengers between London and Paris. In addition to producing aircraft, de Havilland manufactured airplane engines. The first was the four-cylinder Gipsy in 1927.

**DE HAVILLAND COMET.** The first jet airliner put into regular passenger service, starting in 1952. Between May 1953 and April 1954, though, there were three crashes that were later found to have been caused by metal fatigue, so all the craft were grounded.

The improved Comet 4 became a very popular and widely used medium-range plane and in October 1958, became the first jet to be used on the New York–to–London run. The Comet 4 had four Avon engines, each producing 10,500 pounds (4,760 kg) of thrust. Its top speed was 550 mph (885 kph), and the range was 4,000 miles (6,436 km). (Wingspan, 115 feet [35 m]; length, 93 feet 1 inch [28 m].)

**DE HAVILLAND DH 4.** A two-seat braced biplane (1917) that was the best-known high performance day bomber of World War I. Most of the fuselage was wooden with fabric covering. Different models had different engines, but the DH 4s that were equipped with 12-cylinder Rolls-Royce Eagle engines achieved the greatest fame. The pilot's cockpit was located under the top wing; the gunner's cockpit was far aft. This wide separation made communication during combat virtually impossible. The DH 4 carried heavy armament, including one or two Vickers guns for the pilot and a ring-mounted Lewis gun for the gunner. The bombs, which were transported in carriers under the wings and fuselage, were released by the pilot. At 15,000 feet (4,570 m), the aircraft had a maximum speed of 126 mph (202 kph). (Wingspan, 42 feet 5 inches [13 m]; length, 30 feet 2 inches [9 m].)

**DE HAVILLAND DH 60 MOTH.** Designed by Captain De Havilland in 1925, this two-seater biplane was considered the leading light aircraft in the world until the 1930s. It became very popular among the members of the many flying clubs in Great Britain. In 1927 De Havilland produced an engine for the Moth, called the Gipsy, that became standard. Many record flights and acrobatic feats were made with this plane. Best known is Amy Johnson's 1930 record flight.from England to Australia in 195 days, the first Engand-to-Australia solo flight by a woman. (Wingspan, 29 feet [9 m]; length, 23 feet 6 inches [7 m].)

**DE HAVILLAND DH 98 MOSQUITO.** A propeller bomber that was made by Great Britain's De Havilland factory starting in 1940, and was used by the Royal Air Force during World War II. When the Mosquito first went into service, it was the fastest military plane in the world, capable of flying almost 400 mph (644 kph).

The Mosquito aircraft was made of wood and was designed to serve as a light bomber, carrying up to 4,000 pounds (1,800 kg) of bombs. These bombers made some of the most daring raids of the war, including a daylight attack on Cologne.

Later models of this plane served as fighters and were used for reconnaissance. The fighter aircraft carried the heaviest armament of any plane in the war. The Mark 6 was armed with four 20-mm cannons and four machine guns. Nearly eight thousand Mosquitoes were manufactured before the aircraft became obsolete. (Wingspan, 54 feet 2 inches [16 m]; length, 44 feet 6 inches [14 m].)

**DELTA AIR LINES.** One of the largest American domestic airlines. Delta Air Lines originated as the world's first commercial crop-dusting service in 1924. In June 1929 the company began to carry passengers between Atlanta and Birmingham. As it grew, it extended its routes. Today Delta flies mainly in the eastern half of the United States.

**DELTA WING.** A triangularly shaped wing of an aircraft, resembling the shape of the Greek letter "delta" Δ. One of the chief advantages of the large swept-back leading edge of the wing is that it reduces takeoff and landing speeds without the need for flaps. Examples of the delta-wing aircraft are the Convair F 102 Delta Dagger and the Dassault Mirage.

**An Avro Vulcan bomber, a delta-wing aircraft**

**DIRIGIBLE.** Early airship driven by a powerful engine. Like balloons, dirigibles were kept aloft by a gas that was lighter than air. Large dirigibles once carried passengers across the Atlantic in regular service. Between 1910 and 1914, an airline operated by Ferdinand von Zeppelin, the inventor of the dirigible, carried more than thirty-five thousand passengers without a single fatality.

Then, on May 6, 1937, the luxurious hydrogen-filled dirigible *Hindenburg* caught fire and exploded over Lakehurst, New Jersey, just as it was completing a voyage from Germany. Afterward, most dirigibles used helium, a safer gas than hydrogen. *See also* AIRSHIP.

**DIVE BOMBER.** A kind of fighter-bomber aircraft that appeared in the late 1920s. The pilot of a dive bomber locates the enemy target and dives at it almost vertically. At a predetermined height the pilot releases the aircraft's bombs and pulls out of the high-speed dive.

**DOOLITTLE, JAMES HAROLD** (b. 1896). An outstanding American pilot who led the first bombing raid on Tokyo on April 18, 1942. With Doolittle in command, 16 B 25s, usually land-based aircraft, took off from the deck of the aircraft carrier U.S.S. *Hornet*. For his daring and heroism, Doolittle was awarded the Congressional Medal of Honor.

**DORNIER DO 217.** Germany's medium bomber of World War II. The aircraft was developed from the slim Do 17, another medium bomber. When fitted with a radar system, the plane served as a night fighter. As a bomber, it was sometimes used to carry the glider and rocket bombs that were used against Allied shipping in the Mediterranean. Early Do 217s had long tail sections that contained air brakes for dive-bombing attacks.

**DORNIER DO J WAL.** A German transport plane (1922), the Wal was important to the development of civil aviation. Durable and versatile, it was built in a number of models. The plane made possible air transport to many remote areas.

In production from 1922 to 1936, the Wal appeared in more than twenty civil and military versions. It was noted for its relatively large size and its metal construction. Its two engines were located one behind the other above the fuselage. Early passenger Wals carried up to twelve people. The enlarged Do R Super Wal of 1926 could carry up to nineteen passengers as fast as 121 mph (195 kph) over a range of up to 621 miles (1,000 km). (Wingspan, 76 feet 2 inches [23 m]; length, 59 feet 9 inches [18 m].)

**DORNIER DO X.** A large flying boat built by Dornier in France. At the time of its first flight in July 1929, it was the world's largest aircraft. (Wingspan, 157 feet 6 inches [48 m]; length, 133 feet [41 m].)

**DOUGLAS AIRCRAFT COMPANY.** Founded at Santa Monica, California, in 1920, the company's early products included biplane torpedo bombers and a flying boat. The experimental DC-1 airliner of 1933 led to the outstanding series of commercial DC aircraft. In 1967 Douglas Aircraft became part of McDonnell Douglas.

**DOUGLAS A-1. SKYRAIDER.** An attack plane and bomber, the 1945 Skyraider was intended to go out of production in 1950, but its manufacture continued much longer due to widespread military use in the Korean and Vietnam wars. The aircraft took off from land or carrier and was used as a strike aircraft for ground support, antisubmarine, and bombing missions. A single propeller plane powered by one 2,700 hp Wright engine, the aircraft could reach a top speed of 310 mph (500 kph), a ceiling of 28,500 feet (8,687 m), and had a 1,143-mile (1,839-km) range. (Wingspan, 50 feet 9 inches [15 m]; length, 40 feet 1 inch [12 m].)

**DOUGLAS DC-3.** This twin-engine propeller aircraft was probably the most important plane in the early history of American commercial aviation. In production from 1935 until 1946, a total of 10,929 DC-3s were made. A number are still in use by various airlines around the world.

The DC-3 was famous for its safety, speed, reliability, low fuel consumption, and comfort. During World War II, military models were constructed.

With two Pratt & Whitney engines of 1,200 hp each, the DC-3 has a cruising speed of 207 mph (333 kph). Its range is up to 2,125 miles (3,420 km), and it can fly at a 29,000-foot (8,839-m) ceiling. (Wingspan, 95 feet [29 m]; length, 64 feet 5 inches [19 m].)

**DOUGLAS DC-10.** One of the workhorses of today's commercial airlines, the DC-10 was first flown in 1970. The aircraft has three Pratt & Whitney turbofan jet engines, one at the base of the tail and one under each wing. DC-10s have been implicated in a number of air accidents, including the crash on May 25, 1979, that took the lives of 271 on board and two on the ground. The crash was the United States' worst air disaster. DC-10s carry a maximum of about four hundred passengers and cruise at 600 mph (965 kph). (Wingspan, 165 feet [50 m]; length, 181 feet 5 inches [55 m].)

**DOUGLAS DAUNTLESS.** A dive bomber that went into production in 1944. This two-seater aircraft is credited with sinking more Japanese ships than any other Allied weapon and turning the tide of the war in the Pacific.

**DOUGLAS WORLD CRUISERS.** Four World Cruisers, called the *Seattle*, *Chicago*, *Boston*, and *New Orleans*, were built by the Douglas Aircraft Corporation during the early 1920s. Each of these biplanes had a single 400 hp Liberty engine and a wingspan of 50 feet (15 m). Each could fly either with wheels for overland flights or with seaplane floats. All four started out to make the first flight around the world, but only the *Chicago* and the *New Orleans* completed the trip in 1924. It took them 175 days to fly 26,345 miles (42,389 km).

**DRAG.** Resistance of the air to the movement of an aircraft through it.

**DRONE.** An aircraft that flies without a pilot and that is used for target practice with guns or missiles, for research purposes such as air sampling, or for observation and reconnaissance. Drones are controlled from a ground station or by equipment in another aircraft.

# E

**EAGLE SQUADRONS.** A name given to a group of three American-manned squadrons within the British RAF before the United States entered World War II. The Eagle Squadrons were reputed to have destroyed more than seventy enemy aircraft. By late 1944 most of the Eagle Squadrons' fliers had returned to the United States.

**EARHART, AMELIA** (1897–1937). The first woman to fly across the Atlantic alone. She piloted a Lockheed Vega from Grace Harbour, Newfoundland, to Ireland on May 20 and 21, 1932. Earhart is credited with a number of other honors: first woman passenger on a transatlantic flight, first woman to fly across the United States alone both ways, and first woman to receive the Distinguished Flying Cross. On June 1, 1937, Earhart and her copilot, Fred Noonan, left Miami in a two-engine Electra in an attempt to fly around the world at the equator. The plane disappeared at sea while heading for Howland Island in the South Pacific on July 2, 1937.

**EASTERN AIR LINES.** One of the largest of the United States airlines. Founded in 1928, it took its present name in 1938. In number of planes and passengers, EAL ranks close to the top among the world's airlines. In addition to routes in the United States, the company's planes fly to Mexico, Canada,

Bermuda, and Puerto Rico. A special EAL service, the air shuttle, has flown regular, frequent flights between New York and Boston, and New York and Washington, D.C., since 1961.

**EJECTION CAPSULE.** A cockpit that can be expelled from an aircraft in an emergency. The capsule is usually equipped with food and supplies and can serve as shelter after landing safely by parachute on the ground or sea.

**EJECTION SEAT.** An airplane seat that is automatically expelled from a plane in an emergency, freeing the occupant of the aircraft at a safe altitude, so that he or she can use a parachute. Also called ejector seat.

**ELEVATOR.** The hinged, horizontal surfaces at the back edge of the stabilizer that control the pitch of the airplane. By moving the control stick forward the pilot lowers the elevators, raising the direction of flight. Pulling the stick back raises the elevators, causing the plane to descend.

**EMILY.** A code name given by the Allies to the Japanese navy's four-engine fighter plane Kawanishi H8K. The aircraft was the fastest flying boat to see combat in World War II.

**F-4F.** *See* GRUMMAN F-4F WILDCAT.

**F-8.** *See* CHANCE VOUGHT F-8 CRUSADER.

**F-14.** *See* GRUMMAN F-14 TOMCAT.

**F-16.** *See* GENERAL DYNAMICS F-16 FIGHTING FALCON.

**F-27.** *See* FOKKER F-27 FRIENDSHIP.

**F-102.** *See* CONVAIR F-102 DELTA DAGGER.

**F-111.** *See* GENERAL DYNAMICS F-111.

**F-VII.** *See* FOKKER F VII.

**FAA (FEDERAL AVIATION ADMINISTRATION).** This U.S. government agency controls civil aviation in the United States. It is responsible for certification of aircrew and of airplane worthiness. In addition, it is authorized to allocate funds for airport improvements and planning projects and to control noise and air pollution by aircraft.

**FAI (FÉDÉRATION AÉRONAUTIQUE INTERNATIONALE).** An international body formed in 1905 to supervise and establish aviation records and control sport flying. Today the FAI includes fifty countries. It oversees balloon, sailplane, and parachute events, as well as those for powered airplanes.

**A 1911 Farman plane**

**FARMAN.** One of the largest French aircraft manufacturers. The company was founded by brothers Henri and Maurice Farman. In 1907 Henri had established the world speed record of 32.73 mph (52.66 kph) and the distance record of 2,530 feet (711 m). In 1912 he and his brother started the company in which they built and designed planes that were trainers and reconnaissance aircraft during the early years of World War I. Farman aircraft often looked ungainly and boxlike, but were renowned for carrying heavy loads over great distances.

**FARMAN GOLIATH.** This propeller airliner (1919) was one of the first commercial passenger planes to enter service in Europe. The Goliath could carry twelve passengers seated on wicker chairs in two cabins. A crew of two piloted the plane from an open cockpit. About 60 biplane Goliaths were built and used on the Paris to London service and between other European cities. (Wingspan, 86 feet 10 inches [27 m]; length, 47 feet [14 m]).

**FIGHTER.** An aircraft built to attack other planes in the air. During World War I, pilots of opposing observation craft fired at each other with rifles and revolvers. Newer aircraft were equipped with machine guns and cannon. Today's fighters also include air-to-air missiles in their armaments. Most fighters are identified by the letter F and a number.

**FLAPS.** Devices that are fitted to the back, trailing edges of an aircraft's wings to improve handling at low speeds. Lowering or extending the flaps increases the lift that the wing is able to provide. As a result, stalling speed is lowered and landing speed is reduced. The use of flaps on takeoff increases lift and permits a steep ascent.

**FLIGHT SIMULATOR.** A full-size model of a cockpit used for pilot training. The flight simulator contains all the flight instruments and controls usually found in the aircraft. But instead of being used to fly the plane, they are connected to a computer. The computer simulates, or imitates, actual flight as the pilot uses the various controls. The computer even shows views of airports and other features of the terrain the pilot ordinarily sees through the windows. The views change in response to the pilot's handling of the controls.

**FLOATPLANE.** A seaplane that has a pair of long floats or pontoons mounted below the fuselage or wings for operation from water. *See also* SEAPLANE.

**FLYER.** *See* WRIGHT FLYER.

**FLYING BEDSTEAD.** The name given to the first Vertical Take-off and Landing (VTOL) aircraft. Made by Rolls Royce, the plane did indeed look like a four-poster bed. *See also* VTOL.

**FLYING BOAT.** A seaplane in which the fuselage actually makes contact with the water. The first flying boat was designed by Glenn Curtiss in 1911. Flying boats were used for the early transpacific passenger routes. Since 1950 the use of flying boats has decreased because of the air drag caused by the bulky hulls and the provision of airport landing places throughout the world. *See also* SEAPLANE.

**FLYING FORTRESS.** *See* BOEING B-17 FLYING FORTRESS.

**FLYING TIGER LINE.** The world's third largest airfreight carrier. Formed in 1945, the airline assumed its present name in 1946 because its founders had flown with the Flying Tigers over China during World War II. *See also* FLYING TIGERS.

**FLYING TIGERS.** The name given to a group of American volunteers formed to assist China before America entered World War II. The idea originated with Claire Lee Chennault, a retired American officer, who served as air adviser to the Chinese. In June 1942 the Flying Tigers were absorbed into the U.S. Army

Air Force as the 23rd Fighter Group. The company operated in China, Burma, and India until the end of the war.

**FOKKER, ANTHONY HERMAN GERARD** (1890–1939). A Dutch engineer who designed and built monoplanes in the years just before World War I. Fokker established an aircraft manufacturing plant near Berlin, Germany, in 1912. His factories provided Germany with many aircraft which they used in air warfare. Some Fokker planes were equipped with interrupter gear, allowing the machine gun to fire through the spinning propeller. This made the Fokker fighters among the most formidable fighters of World War I. After the war was over, Fokker returned to his native Holland. He set up plants in the Netherlands and later in the United States.

**FOKKER BIRD OF PARADISE.** The first plane to be flown nonstop from California to Hawaii on June 28–29, 1927. Navigational instruments were used successfully for the first time on the historic flight. Albert Hegenberger and Lester Maitland were the navigator and pilot for the 25 hours and 50 minutes of the 2,418-mile (3,891-km) flight.

**FOKKER D VII.** A propeller aircraft (1918) that many American pilots considered the best German fighter of World War I. Built with a strong tubular steel frame, the plane achieved a top speed of 117 mph (188 kph). The single pilot had twin machine guns as armament. (Wingspan, 29 feet 3 inches [9 m]; length, 23 feet [7 m].)

**FOKKER E I EINDECKER.** A propeller fighter that became famous when used by Germans in World War I to destroy a French airplane on July 1, 1915. It was equipped with a machine gun that was synchronized to fire with the revolutions of the propeller. The E III version which was most widely used had two or three machine guns. The Eindecker's usefulness was short-lived, however. The advent of the DH 2 and the Nieuport Scout early in 1916 put an end to the so-called Fokker Scourge. By August 1916 only a few Fokker E Is were still in use. (Wingspan, 31 feet 3 inches [10 m]; length, 23 feet 8 inches [7 m].)

**FOKKER F VII.** This triple-engine airliner (1925) was used for several famous flights by early figures in aviation history. On May 9, 1926, the F VII, equipped with a ski undercarriage, was used in the first flight of Richard E. Byrd and Floyd Bennett over the North Pole. This aircraft was powered by a single 360 hp Rolls Royce Eagle engine. (Wingspan, 63 feet 4 inches (19 m].)

One modification of the F VII made the first flight across the Pacific Ocean from May 31 to June 10, 1928, piloted by Charles Kingsford-Smith. Called the *Southern Cross*, it flew from Oakland, California, to Brisbane, Australia, a distance of 7,389 miles (11,889 km), in 83 hours, 11 minutes, with only two stops, in Hawaii and Fiji. (Wingspan, 71 feet 3 inches [22 m]; length, 47 feet 7 inches [15 m].)

**FOKKER F-27 FRIENDSHIP.** A safe, economical turboprop airliner intended for short-haul services. Put into production in 1955, it has been manufactured ever since because of its high productivity and low cost of operation. (Wingspan, 95 feet 2 inches [29 m]; length, 77 feet 3 inches [23 m].)

**FORD TRIMOTOR.** An all-metal, high-wing, monoplane airliner with corrugated fuselage and very simple interior. This sturdy and very popular aircraft was first made in 1926. One famous Trimotor, nicknamed the *Tin Goose*, remained in service for forty years. A specially adapted Trimotor was used by Richard E. Byrd for the first flight to the South Pole. (Wingspan, 74 feet [23 m]; length, 49 feet 10 inches [15 m].)

**FUEL.** A substance burned to provide heat or power. Kerosene and gasoline are the two fuels for jet engines, and high octane gas is used for the piston engines of propeller planes.

**FUSELAGE.** The main body of an aircraft. The wings, tailplane, and undercarriage are attached to the fuselage. The early aircraft lacked a fuselage, but, as more protection for the pilot was needed, the fuselage evolved into a major part of airplane construction. Before 1915 fuselage construction was almost always of wood. That year the German firm of Junkers built the J 1, the first all-metal aircraft. During the 1930s Duralumin, an aluminum alloy, was used. In recent decades, plastic and fiberglass have been used for light planes, with titanium and other special metals for high-speed aircraft.

# G

**GENERAL AVIATION.** The use of aircraft for agricultural, police, business, recreational, photographic, and medical purposes.

**GENERAL DYNAMICS F-16 FIGHTING FALCON.** This jet fighter (1974) is one of the outstanding military aircraft of modern times. Its top speed is more than Mach 2. Power comes from a single Pratt & Whitney engine, with the air intake located under the fuselage. Despite its great speed, it is also the most maneuverable craft. The F-16 features an electronic control system, so pilots refer to it as a "fly-by-wire" plane. The F-16 can carry up to 15,200 pounds (6,895 kg) of bombs, along with missiles, and a 20 mm cannon. (Wingspan, 31 feet [10 m]; length, 47 feet 8 inches [15 m]).

**GENERAL DYNAMICS F-111.** A jet fighter (1967) that is the world's first aircraft to feature swing-wing design. It serves with the U.S. Air Force as a long-range attack fighter, strategic bomber, and reconnaissance aircraft. The F-111 is powered by two Pratt & Whitney engines of 20,000 pounds (9,072 kg) of thrust. (Wingspan, 63 feet [19 m]; length, 73 feet 6 inches [22 m].)

**GENTILE, DON, AND GODFREY, JOHN.** A team of American aces who together destroyed or damaged thirty enemy aircraft in March 1944 during

World War II. Gentile is credited with twenty-three air victories and seven planes destroyed on the ground, while Godfrey is credited with eighteen in the air and twelve on the ground.

**GLIDER.** *See* SAILPLANE.

**GRAF ZEPPELIN.** The airship that is considered the most successful of its kind. From the time it was put into service in 1928 until it was retired in 1937, the craft carried more than thirteen thousand passengers more than one million miles (1.6 million km) in nearly six hundred trips without one accident. On each flight, the crew, numbering between forty and fifty, and about twenty passengers traveled in a cabin beneath the body of the *Graf Zeppelin*. Before it began regular service between Europe and America, the airship made one round-the-world flight and several trips from Germany to South America, Russia, the Mediterranean, and the Arctic. The airship was 776 feet 3 inches (237 m) long and had five propellers driven by five 560 hp engines.

**GROUND CONTROLLED APPROACH (GCA).** A landing procedure in which traffic controllers on the ground guide the pilot down. The controllers follow the pilot's flight on a radar screen and tell the flyer the proper heading, height, and speed to come in for a safe landing.

**Ground controlled approach**

**GRUMMAN F-4F WILDCAT.** This basic fighter (1940) was used by the U.S. Navy for carrier operation during the early years of World War II. A propeller-driven plane that used a 1,200 hp engine, the aircraft had a top speed of 335 mph (539 kph). The armaments consisted of either four or six .50 machine guns mounted on the wings. Although it was slower than many enemy fighter planes, the Wildcat was often the victor in battle due to its superior firepower and its use of diving passes. Eight thousand Wildcats were produced before 1943, when the plane was retired. (Wingspan, 38 feet [12 m]; length, 28 feet 10 inches [9 m]).

**GRUMMAN F-14 TOMCAT.** A jet fighter (1970) that became the U.S. Navy's first aircraft with swing, or variable, wings. The wings are extended during takeoff and landing, but swing back to cut air drag while in flight. Swing wings allow pilots to slow their approach speeds to permit all-weather deck landings on carrier ships. Two jet engines of 20,900 pounds (9,480 kg) thrust each give the craft a top speed of Mach 2.34 at 40,000 feet (12,200 m). The two-seater Tomcat is armed with air-to-air missiles and a 20 mm cannon. (Wingspan, 64 feet [20 m] extended; 33 feet [10 m] swept back; length 62 feet 7 inches [19 m].)

**GRUMMAN TBF-1 AVENGER.** THE U.S. Navy used this torpedo bomber for twelve years, starting in 1942. Launched from aircraft carriers, this powerfully built plane was the largest of its kind. The Avenger had a 1,900 hp Wright engine, and reached a top speed of 270 mph (430 kph). A crew of three included pilot, gunner, and bombardier. Nearly ten thousand Avengers were built, a thousand of which were used by Britain's Royal Navy. (Wingspan, 54 feet [17 m]; length, 40 feet [13 m].)

**HARTMANN, ERICH "BUBI"** (b. 1922). The top German Ace of World War II, with 352 victories to his credit. Hartmann ranks as the most successful fighter pilot in the history of air warfare. After joining the Luftwaffe in 1940, Hartmann spent most of his war career on the Russian front. On July 7, 1943, he brought down seven Russian aircraft in a single day. His last victory was scored on the last day of the war, May 8, 1945. Hartmann was turned over to the Russians after he surrendered to the American forces. Known as the "Black Devil of the the Ukraine," the pilot was sentenced to ten years imprisonment as a war criminal. After his release, he returned to West Germany and became a jet pilot in the Luftwaffe.

**HAWKER HURRICANE.** The British Royal Air Force's first monoplane fighter, first used in 1935. The Hurricane played a big part in the Battle of Britain, a World War II battle fought in the air between the German Luftwaffe and the Royal Air Force. The tough Hurricane destroyed so many German bombers that the Luftwaffe stopped its mass attacks.

The first Hurricanes had four guns, all of them in the wings. Later versions carried up to twelve guns. The plane was easily repaired and remained in production until late 1944. Its 1,030 hp Rolls Royce engine gave the propeller-driven aircraft a top speed of about 330 mph (531 kph) at 22,000 feet (6,706 m). (Wingspan, 40 feet [12 m]; length; 32 feet [10 m].)

**HAWKER SIDDELEY HARRIER.** The first practical VTOL (Vertical Take Off and Landing) fighter. The Harrier is able to fly vertically by deflecting the thrust of its two jet engines. It also has jet nozzles in the nose, tail, and wing tips so it can maneuver while hovering in the air. Recent models of the aircraft have two Pegasus jet engines, each producing 21,500 pounds (9,740 kg) of thrust. They are armed with two 30 mm cannons and Sidewinder air-to-air missiles, and they can carry up to 3,000 pounds (1,360 kg) of bombs. (Wingspan, 25 feet 3 inches [8 m]; length, 45 feet 6 inches (14 m].)

**HAWKER SIDDELEY TRIDENT.** The three jet engines of this British made airliner (1962) are located on the sides and base of the T-shaped tail of the aircraft. It is a short- to medium-range craft, with a range of about 1,500 miles (2,414 km). The passenger capacity is 103. Later models of the Trident could carry as many as 179 people. Each of the three engines puts out 11,400 pounds (5,160 kg) of thrust. (Wingspan, 98 feet [30 m]; length, 131 feet 2 inches [40 m].)

**HEAD-UP DISPLAY (HUD).** A way of projecting a radar display onto the windshield of a fighter aircraft, so the crew members can determine their position and direction of flight while watching the enemy planes. HUD was developed by British pilots and engineers in 1940.

**HEAT BARRIER.** Heat created by friction between the aircraft and the surrounding air when the plane is flying at speeds of Mach 2 and above. At speeds of Mach 6 the plane's metal skin reaches temperatures of more than 1,000° F (538° C) on the nose and the leading edges of the wings.

**HEINKEL HE 111.** Originally built in Germany in 1935 as an airliner, the airplane had only ten seats, making it uneconomical to fly. During the Spanish Civil War (1936–1939) the He 111 found use as a bomber by the German forces fighting in Spain. In World War II, the He 111 became the standard German medium bomber. Many were lost, but, because there was no better replacement, production continued until 1944, with more than seven thousand manufactured. (Wingspan, 74 feet 1 inch [23 m]; length, 53 feet 9 inches [16 m].)

**HELICOPTER.** A powered aircraft without fixed wings. The helicopter gets its lift and forward motion from the horizontal rotor blades that spin over the body of the craft. Rotor blades are usually powered by a gas turbine engine. Helicopters are used for short-range passenger transport and for law enforcement, agricultural, and medical purposes. In warfare, helicopters are equipped as attack craft, as well as troop carriers.

**HINDENBURG.** One of the most famous airships ever built. The 1936 German-made craft was 804 feet (245 m) long, and held 7 million cubic feet (200,000 m³) of hydrogen. Hydrogen is lighter than air and provided the lift for the airship. The *Hindenburg* was driven forward by four propellers powered by 1,100 hp engines.

The *Hindenburg* made regular crossings between Germany and the United States, carrying up to seventy-five in a compartment beneath the body of the airship. Disaster struck on May 6, 1937, when the *Hindenburg* exploded into flames while approaching her mooring mast at Lakehurst, New Jersey. Thirty-six passengers and crew members were killed. The large number of deaths, coming after some other airship calamities, put an end to large-scale airship travel. *See also* AIRSHIP; DIRIGIBLE.

**The *Hindenburg* explodes.**

**HUGHES, HOWARD** (1905–1976). One of the world's best-known aviators. In 1935 he set a world landplane speed record of 352.46 mph (567 kph) and in 1938 he flew around the world in a record 3 days, 19 hours, and 14 minutes. His all-wood flying boat, nicknamed *Spruce Goose*, had the biggest wingspan of any plane built, 320 feet 6 inches (98 m). It was powered by eight engines. On its single flight November 2, 1947, it flew for less than one mile (1.6 km).

**HYDRAULIC SYSTEM.** A system of pipes and pumps that use a special fluid to operate many of the parts of the plane, such as the landing gear, flaps, rudder, and brakes.

**ICING.** The formation of ice on a plane in flight. Icing can be a serious hazard; it increases weight and drag, reduces lift, and may lock control surfaces. Icing occurs mostly in air with high moisture content and at temperatures between 20° F. and 32° F. Electrical heating is used to prevent icing.

**IFF.** Initials that stand for "Identification, Friend or Foe," an electronic system used in combat to identify hostile aircraft. A plane sends out a radar signal. If the other plane is friendly, it automatically responds with a coded identification reply. If it does not, it is assumed to be an enemy plane.

**ILYUSHIN IL-2 SHTURMOVIK.** A 1941 Russian fighter plane that was specially equipped with air-to-ground rocket projectiles for attacking enemy forces, especially armored vehicles. It was used by Russia against the attacking German forces during World War II. Sergei Ilyushin, who was responsible for the IL-2, was named "Hero of the Soviet Labor" in 1941. About thirty-five thousand IL-2s were built. (Wingspan, 47 feet 10 inches [15 m]; length, 38 feet 1 inch [12 m].)

**IN-FLIGHT REFUELING.** Transferring fuel from one aircraft to another in flight, primarily to increase the range of military aircraft. The first in-flight refueling

**A KC-135
refueling
a B-52H
in flight**

was done by two U.S. Army planes in 1923. The U.S. Air Force introduced in-flight refueling on a large scale in the late 1940s.

**INSTRUMENT LANDING SYSTEM (ILS).** A radio aid that allows a pilot to approach the runway in bad weather. The pilot follows a radio beam transmitted from the airport. ILS is used routinely, even in good visibility.

**ISRAEL AIRCRAFT INDUSTRIES KFIR.** A jet fighter plane produced in Israel in 1975. For many years, the Israeli Air Force had been flying the French Mirage 5 fighter, but in 1967 the French government refused to deliver any more planes to Israel. The Israelis were forced to build their own fighters.

In 1969 they completed the Nesher (Eagle), which was nothing more than a copy of the Mirage 5. Then, in 1975, they produced the superior Kfir (Lion Cub), a very successful military plane. Carrying two 30 mm cannon and four missiles, the one-seater Kfir can fly faster than Mach 2.3 above an altitude of 36,000 feet (11,000 m). It has a ceiling of 52,500 feet (16,000 m). (Wingspan, 27 feet [8 m]; 51 feet [16 m].)

**JABARA, JAMES** (b. 1923). The first American jet fighter ace (WW II) and second highest scoring pilot of the Korean War.

**JENNY.** Jenny was the popular name for the plane officially known as the 1914 Curtiss JN. A two-seater biplane powered by a 90 or 150 hp engine, the Jennies found widespread use as training planes during World War I. Afterward, they were used for training, mail delivery, stunt flying, and general aviation purposes. (Wingspan, 43 feet 7 inches [13 m]; length, 27 feet 4 inches [8 m].

**JET ENGINE.** An aircraft engine that burns liquid fuels, building up pressure in a combustion chamber and then exhausting the gases through its tail pipe. The principle used in jet engines was first stated by Sir Isaac Newton in the year 1687: To every action there is an equal and opposite reaction. It is the pressure of the gases on the front wall of the combustion chamber that drives the plane forward. The force of a jet engine is measured either in pounds (lbs) or kilograms (kgs) of thrust.

A propeller provides thrust by forcing a small volume of air back at a slow speed. The top speed of a propeller-driven plane is about 550 mph (885 kph). A jet engine, however, produces thrust by moving a volume of gas at a very high speed. That is why the jet aircraft must fly fast in order to operate well. The fastest jet can fly more than 2,000 mph (3,218 kph).

The early development of the jet engine took place in England. In 1930 Frank Whittle (b. 1907) patented a design for a turbojet engine. Similar experimentation was going on in Germany. In March 1937 Hans Von Ohain (b. 1911), working for the German Heinkel Company, completed the first test-stand jet engine. The Heinkel Company built and flew the first jet engine aircraft in 1939. Two years later, Whittle designed the engine for the first successful turbojet plane.

**JET STREAM.** A narrow current of air that blows from west to east in a wavy pattern around the globe, at heights of between 30,000 feet and 40,000 feet (9,000 m and 12,000 m). High-flying aircraft flying west to east are helped by the jet stream, which usually blows at speeds of more than 100 mph (160 kph). Planes flying in the opposite direction, though, must use extra fuel to maintain speed. There is a danger of storms and turbulence at the margins of the jet stream.

**JOHNSON, AMY** (1903–1941). One of the best known long-distance women aviators of the 1930s. British-born Johnson got her license to fly in July 1929 and became the first woman in Great Britain to qualify as a licensed aircraft engineer a few months later. In 1930 Johnson made the first solo flight by a woman from England to Australia flying the Gipsy Moth *Jason*. Johnson competed in many air races and set many speed records. She was killed on January 5, 1941, when her aircraft crashed into the Thames River.

**JUNKERS F 13.** The first all-metal airliner, this propeller-driven monoplane had a tough, corrugated covering of aluminum alloy. The low-wing planes were in production throughout the 1920s. Used mostly for commercial purposes, they were a familiar sight throughout Europe after World War I. (Wingspan, 58 feet 3 inches [18 m]; length, 31 feet 6 inches [10 m].)

**JUNKERS J 1.** The first all-metal plane, designed and built in 1916 by Hugo Junkers (1859–1935) for the German military. Although the plane reached speeds up to 100 mph (160 kph), the German High Command was not impressed with the plane, and referred to it as the "Tin Donkey."

Late in 1917, Junkers revamped the original J 1, which became the J 9, armed with two forward-firing guns. The plane was flight-tested by the Red Baron, Manfred von Richthofen. Despite the plane's splendid performance during tests, the High Command rejected it. (Wingspan, 55 feet [17 m]; length, 29 feet 8 inches [9 m].)

**JUNKERS JU 87 STUKA.** The German Luftwaffe's principal dive-bomber used in ground attack raids between 1940 and 1942. The plane was easily recognizable by its W-shaped wings, big undercarriage, and angular tail surfaces.

Specially designed for dive-bombing, Stukas were fitted with sirens to produce a screaming howl as they dived and dropped bombs on ground targets. Their pilots called the Stukas the "trombones of Jericho." (Wingspan, 45 feet 3 inches [14 m]; length, 36 feet 5 inches [11 m].)

**JUNKERS JU 88.** Germany's most effective bomber used during World War II. The original 1936 model had two propellers driven by 1,200 hp engines, and a top speed of 286 mph (460 kph). A number of different versions of the JU 88 were produced for dive bombing, torpedo bombing, reconnaissance, and night fighting. It is estimated that more than fifteen thousand planes of this type were manufactured. (Wingspan, 62 feet [19 m]; length, 51 feet [16 m].)

**KAMIKAZE.** Members of the Japanese air force who performed the suicide mission of crashing explosive-laden aircraft into enemy targets during World War II. Many of the twenty-nine hundred Kamikaze sorties were flown during the defense of Okinawa in April 1945. The usual Kamikaze attacker was the Zero fighter plane. The word *kamikaze* literally means "Divine Wind." It refers to a gale which scattered the ships of an attacking fleet of Mongols in 1281.

**KAZAKOV, ALEXANDER** (1889–1919). During World War I, this pilot became Russia's top-scoring air ace. He achieved seventeen confirmed victories and is credited with thirty-two kills. Kazakov died in a mysterious flying accident.

**KFIR.** *See* ISRAEL AIRCRAFT INDUSTRIES KFIR.

**KOMET.** *See* MESSERSCHMITT ME 163 KOMET.

**LANCASTER.** *See* AVRO LANCASTER.

**LANGLEY, SAMUEL PIERPONT** (1834–1906). The first American to attempt sustained, powered flight. In 1898 Langley was asked by the Federal government to investigate the possible uses of man-carrying aircraft in war. He failed twice in 1903; the second failure, on December 8, came only nine days before the Wright brothers' successful flight at Kitty Hawk.

**LIFT.** A force exerted by an airflow that opposes the pull of gravity. The top surface of an aircraft's wing is curved, so that air passing above the wing moves faster than the air passing beneath. According to Bernoulli's Law, the greater the air speed, the lower the air pressure. Air pressure of the slow-moving air under the wing is greater than the air pressure of the fast-moving air above the wing. Thus, an upward force, or lift, is created.

**LIGHT AIRCRAFT.** A term for all aircraft that weigh less than 12,500 pounds. (5,670 kg). In the early 1930s, light racing planes were especially popular in America. Even today, American light aircraft predominate in the world market. Cessnas and Pipers have been especially successful. The aircraft use piston engines because of the efficiency of propellers at low speeds.

**Otto Lilienthal
attempting flight**

**LILIENTHAL, OTTO** (1848–1896). A German pioneer aviator whose experiments with manned gliders helped make the powered airplane possible. Most of Lilienthal's machines resembled today's hang gliders. He launched himself from a hill and hung onto the glider with his shoulders and arms. Steering was accomplished by swinging the body and legs. Over a period of five years, Lilienthal made more than two thousand flights. On August 9, 1896, he went into a dive, broke his back, and died the next day. Some credit Lilienthal's experiments with inspiring the Wright brothers.

**LINDBERGH, CHARLES AUGUSTUS** (1902–1974). An American aviator who made the first solo crossing of the Atlantic. Lindbergh began his flying career as a stunt flyer with a World War I Curtiss *Jenny*, earning the nickname "Daredevil." He decided to try for the $25,000 prize offered for the first New York-to-Paris nonstop crossing. He made the flight on May 20–21, 1927, in a single-engine Ryan monoplane named *Spirit of St. Louis*. The flight covered a distance of 3,610 miles (5,809 km) and lasted thirty-three and a half hours. It made Lindbergh an instant hero. He and his wife, Anne Morrow, made many additional pioneering flights in the 1930s.

In 1932, the Lindberghs' infant son was kidnapped and murdered. The couple left the country and went to live in Europe. Before the outbreak of World War II, Lindbergh supported neutrality for America and lost his popularity. But after the United States entered the war, Lindbergh supported his country.

**Charles Lindbergh**

**LOCKHEED C-5A GALAXY.** One of the largest airplanes in the world. The 1968 jet transport can carry 265,000 pounds (120,200 kg) of cargo. For loading large objects into the 19 foot by 121 foot (6 m by 37 m) cargo area, the entire nose of the Galaxy tilts up. Above the cargo space is a second deck with seventy-three seats. The crew quarters have room for a six-person crew, a relief crew of six, and eight couriers.

The Galaxy is powered by four General Electric turbofan jets mounted on pylons beneath the wings. Each one puts out 41,000 pounds (18,600 kg) of thrust. The top speed is 550 mph (885 kph); range is 6,500 miles (10,460 km). (Wingspan, 222 feet 8 inches [68 m]; length, 247 feet 10 inches [76 m].)

**LOCKHEED C-130 HERCULES.** The long-range workhorse of air transport. Pilots say it is "built like a truck, but handles like a Cadillac." This 1954 giant aircraft can carry up to 44,000 pounds (19,958 kg) of freight, or ninety-two fully loaded troops.

The Hercules requires less than 300 yards (274 m) for takeoff and for landing. A Hercules has even taken off and landed on the deck of the aircraft carrier *U.S.S. Forestal.* Hercules has four propellers, each powered by a 4,000 hp Allison turboprop engine. The top speed is 360 mph (580 kph); the ceiling, 23,000 feet (7,010 m). Hercules has a range, fully loaded, of about 4,700 miles (7,562 km). (Wingspan, 132 feet 7 inches [40 m]; length, 97 feet 9 inches [30 m].)

**LOCKHEED CONSTELLATION.** This plane was first conceived in 1939, when TWA asked Lockheed to design a new long-range passenger aircraft. At the outbreak of World War II, plans were revised and a military plane, the C-69 military transport, was developed instead.

After the war, work was resumed on the civilian model, and a Constellation with sixty seats was built in 1946. It was bought by airlines all around the world. Further improvements were made over the following years, until 1950, when the Super Constellation was announced. Various features were upgraded, and, in 1956, the Starliner was produced. Altogether 856 Constellations of the different types were made. The top cruising speed was 323 mph (520 kph); the range, 5,400 miles (8,690 km). (Wingspan, 150 feet [46 m]; length, 113 feet 7 inches [35 m].)

**LOCKHEED ELECTRA.** An elegant all-metal passenger transport aircraft (1934) that was. laid out for two pilots and ten passengers. The Electra was easy to recognize because of its two tail fins and retractable undercarriage. The inside of the wing covering was corrugated.

The Electra reached a maximum speed of 200 mph (320 kph). Amelia Earhart, one of the most famous aviators of the 1930s, was flying an Electra on an attempted round-the-world flight when she disappeared in 1937. (Wingspan, 55 feet [17 m]; length, 38 feet 7 inches [12 m].)

**LOCKHEED L-1011 TRISTAR.** One of the most popular modern jumbo-jet airliners, introduced in 1970. Two of the TriStar's engines are located beneath the wings, and one is in the tail. Each engine produces 42,000 pounds (19,050 kg) of thrust. The cruising speed is 562 mph (904 kph), and, with the extra fuel capacity of later models, the range is up to 6,100 miles (9,815 km). TriStars can carry up to four hundred passengers. (Wingspan, 155 feet 4 inches [47 m]; length, 177 feet 8 inches [54 m].)

**LOCKHEED P-38 LIGHTNING.** One of the most successful fighters of World War II. American pilots flying P-38s shot down more Japanese planes than those flying any other plane. The P-38 is most distinctive in appearance. The pilot sits in a pod between the wings. There are two separate narrow bodies, ending in a twin-finned tail, and two propellers. The P-38 could reach speeds of 414 mph (666 kph). (Wingspan, 52 feet [16 m]; length, 37 feet 10 inches [12 m].)

**LOCKHEED SR-71A BLACKBIRD.** A spectacular jet aircraft for reconnaissance and observation purposes, the 1966 SR-71A can reach a maximum altitude of 100,000 feet (30,480 m), and can fly at a speed of Mach 3. The SR-71A set a world speed record of 2,193 mph (3,529 kph), and an altitude record of 86,000 feet (26,213 m). One flew from New York to London in less than two hours.

The aircraft has a unique appearance. The fuselage is thin, flat, and long-nosed. It has delta wings and is equipped with twin fins. The outer covering is made of a special titanium metal alloy. The Blackbird carries a crew of two, one as pilot, the other to operate the reconnaissance systems. Both must wear the same pressurized suits that astronauts do because of the high altitude the Blackbird reaches. (Wingspan, 55 feet 7 inches [17 m]; length, 107 feet 5 inches [33 m].)

**LOCKHEED U-2.** A jet spy plane used to observe enemy troops and facilities, the 1955 U-2 is also used for research and to obtain high-altitude air samples.

**A Lockheed U-2 spy plane**

With 17,000 pounds (7,711 kg) of thrust from a Pratt & Whitney engine, the U-2 has a maximum speed of 495 mph (797 kph) and a ceiling of 70,000 feet (21,000 m). Its maximum range is 4,000 miles (6,436 km).

On May 1, 1960, United States pilot Gary Powers, flying a U-2, was shot down over Russia by a Russian surface-to-air missile. As a result of the furor that followed, the United States agreed not to send any more spy planes into Soviet air space. (Wingspan, 80 feet [24 m]; length, 49 feet 7 inches [15 m].)

**LOCKHEED VEGA.** This beautifully streamlined propeller aircraft of 1927 was built entirely of wood. It was powered by a single engine, had a maximum speed of 135 mph (217 kph), and had a range of about 690 miles (1,110 km).

The most famous of all Vegas was the one owned by an oil magnate, F.C. Hall. It was named *Winnie Mae* after his daughter. Wiley Post, a pilot, flew the *Winnie Mae* around the world on June 23, 1931, in 8 days, 15 hours, and 51 minutes. On July 15, 1933, he circled the world again in almost one day less. In addition to being renowned racing aircraft and record-breakers, Vegas were used successfully by about thirty-six United States domestic airlines. (Wingspan, 41 feet [13 m]; length, 27 feet 6 inches [8 m].)

**LORAN (*Long Range Navigation*).** A navigational system that measures the length of time it takes pulses from separate radio transmitting stations to reach the radio receiver of an aircraft. The time separation between them, in microseconds, helps the pilot or navigator establish the plane's position.

**LUFTWAFFE.** The German Air Force. Established in March 1935, the *Luftwaffe* started with 20,000 men and 1,880 aircraft. By the summer of 1939, on the eve of World War II, the Luftwaffe had 1.5 million men and 3,650 planes. With many initial victories, the Luftwaffe met its first setbacks in the Battle of Britain. After three years of war, it had no reserves, no advanced aircraft designs, and shortages of fuel and pilots. Most of the Luftwaffe planes were grounded.

A new Luftwaffe was established in 1956. Today its personnel number more than 100,000.

**MACH NUMBER.** The ratio of the air speed of a body to the speed of sound at the same altitude. An aircraft that is traveling at the speed of sound is said to be flying at Mach 1. A speed half the speed of sound is Mach 0.5; twice the speed of sound, Mach 2; and so on.

The name of this ratio of air speed to speed of sound comes from the Austrian physicist Ernst Mach (1838–1916), who developed this method for measuring bodies moving at high speeds through gases, such as air.

**MARTIN B-26 MARAUDER.** The fastest medium bomber in the Army Air Forces during World War II. With two propellers driven by 1,850 hp Pratt & Whitney Double Wasp engines, it had a maximum speed of 315 mph (507 kph) and could carry 5,800 pounds (2,631 kg) of bombs. The B-26 had the distinction of being the safest Allied bomber in the war. The Martin Company produced 5,266 B-26s that flew more than 110,000 missions with a combat loss of only one-half of one percent. (Wingspan, 71 feet [22 m]; length, 56 feet 1 inch [17 m].)

**McCONNELL, JOSEPH, JR.** (1922–1954). The highest-scoring American fighter-pilot ace of the Korean War, with a record of sixteen enemy aircraft destroyed.

**McDONNELL DOUGLAS A-4 SKYHAWK.** A very successful jet attack aircraft built in 1954. Used by the U.S. Air Force in the Vietnam War and by the Israelis in the Six-Day war of 1973, it is still flown by the U.S. Marines. The Skyhawk is powered by a Pratt & Whitney engine of 8,500 pound (3,856 kg) thrust. It has a top speed of 675 mph (1,087 kph), and a ceiling of 47,900 feet (14,600 m). In February 1979, after twenty-two years of production and almost three thousand aircraft, manufacture of the Skyhawk ceased. (Wingspan, 27 feet 5 inches [8 m]; length, 41 feet 2 inches [13 m].)

**McDONNELL DOUGLAS F-4 PHANTOM.** The leading fighter plane of the 1960s and early 1970s, with 5,177 manufactured before production stopped in 1979. It is estimated that about 4,000 are still being flown by American and eleven other nations' air forces. The F-4 set new records for speed, climbing power, and high altitude flying.

The Phantom is a two-seater general-purpose fighter plane that was originally built in 1958 by McDonnell Douglas for the U.S. Navy. It has two engines that give it a top speed of 1,584 mph (2,550 kph), and a ceiling of 71,000 feet (21,640 m). The plane can carry up to 16,000 pounds (7,250 kg) of bombs or air-to-surface missiles. The Phantom is fitted with air-to-air missiles and a 20 mm cannon. (Wingspan, 38 feet 5 inches [12 m]; length, 58 feet 3 inches [18 m].)

**McDONNELL DOUGLAS F-15 EAGLE.** One of the fastest and most maneuverable fighters in the world today. First built in 1972, it has two Pratt & Whitney 27,000-pound (12,250-kg) thrust jet engines. The Eagle can climb at Mach 1 and has a top speed of Mach 2.5. The pilot of the F-15 is furnished with a number of missiles and an M-61 cannon. The aircraft can carry up to 14,000 pounds (6,350 kg) of bombs. (Wingspan, 42 feet 10 inches [13 m]; length, 63 feet 10 inches [19 m].)

**MESSERSCHMITT, WILLY** (1898–1978). One of the leading German aircraft designers before and during World War II. By the 1920s, Messerschmitt had built and flown several original plane designs, and in 1923 he established his own aircraft factory. Among other aircraft, it produced the BF 109 fighter, which remained in production throughout World War II. After the war, Messerschmitt worked in Argentina before returning to Germany in the mid-1950s.

**MESSERSCHMITT BF 109.** This single-seat propeller aircraft, first flown in 1935, was used by German Luftwaffe pilots throughout the Spanish Civil War of 1936–39. More of these German fighter planes, an estimated thirty-three thousand, were put into service during World War II than any other aircraft.

Armed with machine guns and cannon, the BF 109s' 1,100 hp engine provided a maximum speed of 357 mph (574 kph). Later models of the BF 109, which were faster and better armed, were used in the great battles of World War II, including the invasions of Poland and France and the Battle of Britain. The aircraft was equipped with a cannon that fired through the hub of the propeller, and two machine guns set in the engine cowling. (Wingspan, 32 feet 7 inches [10 m]; length, 29 feet 4 inches [9 m].)

**MESSERSCHMITT ME 163 KOMET.** The only operational World War II aircraft that used rocket propulsion. The tailless Me 163 was designed as a high-speed research aircraft, but later was developed as an interceptor, armed with two cannon and rocket missiles. The Me 163 B reached a maximum speed of 597 mph (960 kph). While these planes did achieve some success, they were dangerous to fly and accidents were common. (Wingspan, 30 feet 7 inches [9 m]; length, 18 feet 8 inches [6 m].)

**MESSERSCHMITT ME 262.** Originally designed as a propeller-driven fighter plane, the 1941 German-built Me 262 was converted to become the first operational jet aircraft. It was used by the German Luftwaffe as both a bomber and

**A Messerschmitt Me 262**

fighter during World War II. Its top speed was 525 mph (840 kph); its ceiling, 39,360 feet (12,000 m). As a fighter/bomber it carried twenty-four rockets under its wings and two 550-pound (250-kg) bombs. Some models had, in addition, four 30 mm cannons in the nose. (Wingspan, 41 feet [13 m]; length, 34 feet 9 inches [11 m].)

**METAL FATIGUE.** The cracking or breaking apart of metal due to repeated stress. At low stress, metals, such as steel or aluminum, stretch; when the stress is removed, the metal returns to its original size. If there is too much stress, though, the damage is permanent and eventually the metal breaks. Today special care is taken to make aircraft either fatigue-proof or to make it possible to land safely even if there is metal fatigue.

**MIKOYAN MI-12.** A Russian-built helicopter, the Mi-12 (1971) is the largest such aircraft in the world. The twin rotor blades have a diameter of 220 feet (67 m), and are driven by four 6,500 hp engines, for a top speed of 160 mph (257 kph). The Mi-12 is believed able to lift a load of 88,636 pounds (40,200 kg). The plane was first shown at the 1971 Paris Air Show. It has been code-named ''Homer'' by NATO and is considered a military craft, though it may also be used for civilian purposes.

**MIKOYAN MIG-25.** Code-named the ''Foxbat A,'' the MiG-25 is one of the most remarkable fighter planes, designed in 1967 by Artem I. Mikoyan and Mikhail I. Gurevich. The name ''MiG'' combines the first letters of their last names. The power of the MiG-25 comes from two large afterburning jet engines of 25,000 pounds (11,340 kg) thrust each, mounted side-by-side in the rear fuselage. The MiG-25 has a top speed of approximately Mach 3, and a range of 806 miles (1,296 km). Most outstanding is the MiG-25 record for altitude (123,524 feet [37,650 m]) established in 1973, and for speed over a marked course (1,852.5 mph [2,982 kph]) set in 1967. Armament includes four air-to-air missiles. (Wingspan, 45 feet [14 m]; length, 69 feet [21 m].)

**MILITARY TRANSPORT.** Any aircraft used for carrying troops and military equipment. Most military transports are versions of civilian aircraft of their day. During World War II the Allies used the Douglas C-47, a military version of the DC-3, as their workhorse. The main German transport was the Junkers Ju 52/3. An important advance in the development of large transports was the Lockheed Hercules, which was first flown in August 1954. It was a highly efficient and maneuverable aircraft. In recent years, the work of military transport, especially in battlefield situations, has been taken over by large helicopters.

**MIRAGE.** *See* DASSAULT MIRAGE.

**MITSUBISHI A6M ZERO.** The best and most numerous of the Japanese propeller fighters of World War II. This tough 1939 aircraft had excellent handling characteristics and a long range. It dominated the air over the Pacific until early 1943. (Wingspan, 39 feet 4 inches [12 m]; length, 29 feet 9 inches [9 m].)

**MONOCOQUE.** A type of fuselage construction in which the covering on the fuselage carries most or all of the stresses on it. The technique was first used in 1910. Even today's modern thin-winged supersonic aircraft have most of the stresses carried in the strong metal skin.

**MONOPLANE.** An airplane with a single wing extending outward on each side of the body. The majority of aircraft, both civil and military, are monoplanes. Most large and medium-size commercial transports are low-winged. The wing is mounted on the bottom of the fuselage. Most warplanes and light single-engine airplanes are high-winged. The wing is on top of the fuselage.

**MONTGOLFIER BROTHERS.** French inventors of the hot air balloon and builders of the first man-carrying balloon. Joseph Michel Montgolfier (1740–1810) and Jacques Étienne Montgolfier (1745–99) were mill owners who conducted balloon experiments in their spare time. On June 5, 1783, the brothers gave a public demonstration of a hot-air balloon 30 feet (9 m) in diameter. A few months later, at Versailles, they sent aloft a larger balloon that carried a sheep, a duck, and a rooster for a flight that lasted approximately eight minutes. On November 21, 1783, they launched a still larger balloon. The pilot, Pilâtre de Rozier, and passenger, Marquis d'Arlandes, became the first people to leave the earth.

**NAVIGATION.** The science of finding the way from place to place. Today most aircraft follow radio signals beamed into the sky by ground transmitters. Radio receivers in the plane pick up these signals and automatically indicate the direction of the signal. In addition, the pilot has instruments that indicate direction, altitude, and speed, with loran (Long Range Navigation) to determine position and radar to detect the terrain below and any other aircraft.

**NAVY-CURTISS 4.** On May 15, 1919, the NC-4 and two other flying boats attempted a formation flight across the Atlantic. The biplane NC-4 was the only one to complete the trip. It arrived in Lisbon, Portugal, on the morning of May 27, becoming the first airplane to span the Atlantic, even though it made several landings in the water along the way. (Wingspan, top, 126 feet [38 m], bottom, 114 feet [35 m]; length, 68 feet 4 inches [21 m].)

**NESHER.** *See* ISRAEL AIRCRAFT INDUSTRIES.

**NIEUPORT 17.** One of a series of French-made propeller fighters that in 1916 were among the first planes to be used for military fights. So that the propeller blades did not get in the way of the guns, the French mounted the machine gun, pointing at a slightly upward angle, on the center section of the biplane's upper wing.

**NIGHT FIGHTER.** A fighter capable of locating and attacking enemy planes at night by use of radar. Night fighters were slowly developed during World War I in response to night attacks by German bombers over Britain and France. Radar was being used successfully by 1943. One of the best World War II fighters was the De Havilland DH 98 Mosquito. Today almost all fighter aircraft are radar equipped and are able to operate at night or in bad weather.

**NORTH AMERICAN B-1.** In 1970 the Rockwell International Company was asked to design a jet bomber to replace the Boeing B-52. The goal was a high-speed, low-level aircraft that would be able to penetrate enemy radar without detection.

The first flights of the resulting plane, the B-1, were in 1974. The most striking feature about the B-1 is its movable wings, called swing wings. At takeoff and for slow flight, the wings are extended to their full length. For supersonic flight the wings swing back, creating much less air drag. With four General Electric jet engines, each one developing 30,000 pounds (13,608 kg) of thrust, the B-1 can reach speeds of 760 mph (1,223 kph) at low levels, and Mach 2, or more than 1,320 mph (2,124 kph), at high altitudes.

There are four crew members on the B-1, each one with a full set of controls. Also, the plane has a number of computers on board for automatic operation. Although it is much smaller than the B-52, the B-1 can carry about twice as many weapons, including bombs and missiles. The B-1 carries no defensive armament. It depends on its great speed to evade the enemy. (Wingspan, extended, 136 feet 8 inches [42 m], swept back, 78 feet [24 m]; length, 143 feet [44 m].)

**NORTH AMERICAN B-25 MITCHELL.** This propeller bomber (1940) was named after General Billy Mitchell, one of the first to recognize the military importance of air power. The B-25 had two Wright engines that delivered 3,400 hp together, and allowed a highest speed of 322 mph (518 kph). All B-25s could be easily spotted by the two fins on the tail. The aircraft became well known because of its use in the carrier-based raid on Japan led by General James Doolittle during World War II. The Air Corps used a total of about ten thousand B-25s. (Wingspan, 67 feet 7 inches [21 m]; length, 52 feet 11 inches [16 m].)

**NORTH AMERICAN F-86 SABRE.** The original swept-wing jet fighter first used by the U.S. Air Force in 1949. The aircraft saw service in the Korean War against the Russian MiG-15. Although it had a lower ceiling and less climbing ability, the Sabre still proved to be a superior craft. The advanced F-86H had a General Electric turbojet engine with 5,200 pounds (2,359 kg) of thrust that gave it a top speed of more than 700 mph (1,126 kph). Nearly nine thousand Sabres were built.

In 1953 North American introduced the F-100 Super-Sabre. With a Pratt & Whitney engine it had a top speed of 860 mph (1,380 kph). It could carry up to 7,500 pounds (3,400 kg) of bombs or missiles, and was armed with four 20 mm cannon. About twenty-three hundred Super-Sabres were produced. (Wingspan, 37 feet 1 inch [11 m]; length, 37 feet 6 inches [11 m].)

**NORTH AMERICAN X-15.** An experimental rocket-powered aircraft that broke all records for speed and altitude. Between 1959 and 1968, the X-15 achieved a speed of Mach 6.72, which equals 4,534 mph (7,297 kph). Also, the aircraft reached a height of 67.08 miles (108 km). The X-15 was launched in the air from a B-52. Power came from a liquid-fuel rocket that produced 60,000 pounds (27,216 kg) of thrust for a limited period of time. (Wingspan, 22 feet (7 m); length, 52 feet 5 inches [16 m].)

**OHAIN, HANS-JOACHIM PABST VON** (b.1911). A pioneer aircraft engineer who designed the engine used in the world's first jet-powered aircraft, the Heinkel He 178, launched August 27, 1939. After World War II, the German-born Von Ohain came to the United States where he worked on research projects for the government.

**ORNITHOPTER.** A machine with human-powered flapping wings, one of the oldest approaches to human flight. Ornithopters of all kinds have been tried, but none have been successful.

**PAN AMERICAN.** The oldest international airline in the United States, formed in 1927 by Juan T. Trippe. The company soon won a contract from the post office to fly mail between Key West, Florida, and Havana, Cuba. In the 1930s, Pan American pioneered routes to South America and across both the Pacific and Atlantic oceans, mostly with flying boats that were called "flying clippers." By 1945 the flying clippers were replaced by faster and more economical Constellations and DC-4s. The airline was the first to use the 747 in 1970, and in 1976 opened the New York-to-Tokyo route over the North Pole.

**PARACHUTE.** A folding device made out of fabric with cords supporting a harness that allows a person or object to descend safely through the air from an aircraft. The parachute, expanded by air during the descent, is slowed down by air resistance.

Parachutes are used when it is necessary to bail out of a plane, for dropping military personnel and supplies into a strategic location, for braking high-speed aircraft after touchdown, for recovering spacecraft, and for recreation.

The first successful parachute landing was made in 1783. A Frenchman, Louis-Sébastien Lenormand descended from a tower. The first parachute descent from an aircraft was made in 1912 by U.S. Army Captain Albert Berry.

**PAYLOAD.** The number of passengers or amount of freight that an aircraft or spacecraft can carry. Also the explosive charge carried in a missile warhead and the amount of explosives carried by a bomber.

**PEDAL PLANE.** A human-powered plane that is pedaled like a bicycle. A person pedaling two horsepower can develop enough power for takeoff. For the proper lift, wingspans of pedal planes have been as long as 82 feet (25 m). Bryan Allen, an American, set the pedal plane record on June 12, 1979, by flying his craft, the *Gossamer Albatross*, the 22.26 miles (35.82 km) from Folkestone, England, to Cap Gris-Nez, France, in 2 hours and 49 minutes.

**PISTON ENGINE.** The main engine used in powered flight in the early years of aviation, now used primarily for propeller-driven light planes. The piston engine works on the same principle as the modern gasoline automobile engine.

**PITCH.** One of the three basic movements of an aircraft. Pitch refers to the movement of the plane's nose up or down. *See also* ROLL and YAW.

**PITOT TUBE.** A device for measuring air pressure; the measurements are then used to determine the speed of an aircraft. Named after its inventor Henri Pitot (1695–1771), the Pitot tube projects forward into the airflow.

**POST, WILEY** (1899–1935). Pioneer American pilot and the first man to fly around the world alone. At age twenty-five, Post lost an eye in an accident and used the $1,800 compensation money to buy his first airplane. Post set many intercity speed records. He died in an air crash in Alaska, flying with humorist Will Rogers as passenger. His plane, *Winnie Mae*, is now in the aviation collection of the Smithsonian Institution in Washington, D.C.

**PRESSURIZATION.** Increasing the air pressure in aircraft cabins to protect the crew and passengers while flying at high altitudes. The low pressure and lack of oxygen at heights above 10,000 feet (3,048 m) cause discomfort and loss of efficiency; above 20,000 feet (6,096 m) loss of consciousness.

**PROPELLER.** A device with two or more blades extending from a central rotating shaft. The rapidly spinning propeller of an aircraft either pushes or pulls the craft through the air.

**RACING.** Speed competitions were an important part of the early history of aviation. The first big international race was held in 1909, just six years after the Wright brothers' first flight. Glenn Curtiss won with a speed of 47.65 mph (76.68 kph). For the next thirty years there were competitions for a number of prestigious prizes—the James Gordon Bennett Aviation Cup, Schneider Cup, Pulitzer Trophy, Curtiss Marine Flying Trophy, King's Cup, Thompson Trophy, Bendix Trophy, and the U.S. National Air Races. Since the 1940s there has been much less interest in air racing.

**RADAR (*RADIO DETECTION AND RANGING*).** Radar is a method for detecting the location and speed of moving objects and pinpointing fixed objects. Radar can "see" by means of short wave radio waves, just as humans see by means of light waves. Both ground control and the plane's radar send out pulses of radio waves. When the waves strike an object, they are reflected back like echoes. These reflected waves are picked up by a radar antenna and cause dots of light, called blips, to appear on a screen. The air traffic controllers use radar to guide planes in their area. Pilots use radar to locate storms, other planes and aircraft, and landmarks on the terrain over which they are flying.

**RADIAL ENGINE.** An engine commonly used for propeller planes. The cylinders are arranged in a circle around the crankshaft.

**RADIO DIRECTION FINDER.** An aircraft navigation device, consisting of a directional radio antenna that turns to seek the direction of the radio signal, and then guides the plane toward the radio transmitter.

**RANGE.** The distance an aircraft can travel nonstop or without refueling.

**RECONNAISSANCE AIRCRAFT.** A plane designed for observation, usually by the military, to determine the position, strength, and movement of enemy troops in the field or to gather other types of information.

**REPUBLIC F-84 THUNDERJET.** This jet fighter was the main craft flown by the U.S. Air Force in the Korean War and during the 1950s. Advanced models of the 1946 Thunderjet had speeds of around 600 mph (966 kph), using a General Electric turbojet engine. The range was 2,000 miles (3,200 km), but it could be extended with in-flight refueling. Variations on the basic Thunderjet design were the F-84F Thunderstreak, with a swept-wing arrangement, and the RF-84F Thunderflash, which was used for photo reconnaissance. In the twelve years that these planes were manufactured, 4,457 Thunderjets, 2,711 Thunderstreaks, and 715 Thunderflashes were produced. (Wingspan, 36 feet 5 inches [11 m]; length, 38 feet 1 inch [12 m].)

**REPUBLIC P-47 THUNDERBOLT.** A large, heavy, single-seat, propeller fighter plane that was called the "Jug." The 1941 Thunderbolt went through a series of design changes and improvements during the years of World War II. The original plane had a speed of 430 mph (692 kph) and a ceiling of 42,000 feet (12,800 m). Its range, though, was only 550 miles (885 km), and it had poor maneuverability and rate of climb. Later P-47 models had better speed, range, and climbing power. Altogether, more than fifteen thousand Thunderbolts of all models were built. Because of their sturdy construction, fewer than one percent were lost in combat. (Wingspan, 40 feet 9 inches [12 m]; length, 36 feet 1 inch [11 m].)

**RICHTHOFEN, MANFRED VON** (1892–1918). The legendary Red Baron, ace of the German air force during World War I and leader of the "flying circus,'' the most deadly group of fighter pilots in the war. Between September 17, 1916, and April 20, 1918, Richthofen shot down eighty enemy planes. On April 21, 1918, he was forced down and found dead of bullet wounds. It is not certain if he was shot in the air or on the ground.

*Left*: **Manfred Von Richthofen, the Red Baron** *Right*: **Eddie Rickenbacker**

**RICKENBACKER, EDWARD "EDDIE"** (1890–1973). America's ace flyer of World War I and winner of the Medal of Honor. A racing car driver before the war, Rickenbacker enlisted as a staff driver. In August 1917, he transferred to the aviation section, where he learned to fly. By March 1918 he joined the 94th Aero Pursuit Squadron. Before the war was over, he shot down twenty-two enemy planes and four balloons. From 1938 until 1959 he was president of Eastern Air Lines.

**ROCKET.** A type of engine, similar to the jet, that produces its forward thrust by means of exhaust gases that rush out the rear. In both rockets and jets a fuel is burned to create the gases. Rockets supply their own oxygen for the combustion; jets get their oxygen from the air. Rockets can, therefore, fly into outer space where there is no oxygen, and are used to power space shots. Jets cannot leave the earth's atmosphere.

There have been a few experimental rocket-powered planes. In 1962 Major Robert M. White of the U.S. Air Force set an altitude record of 60 miles (96 km) for flight in a rocket-powered North American X-15-1.

**ROLL.** One of the three basic movements of an aircraft. Roll refers to the rising or dipping of the plane's wings. *See also* PITCH and YAW.

**ROTARY ENGINE.** A type of radial engine in which the block containing the cylinders rotates to drive the propeller. Rotary engines were popular in planes before 1920.

**RYAN SPIRIT OF ST. LOUIS.** The single-seater plane flown by Charles A. Lindbergh (1902–1974) on his first solo flight across the Atlantic Ocean on May 20–21, 1927. The flight took thirty-three and a half hours.

The *Spirit of St. Louis* was a Ryan monoplane with a 237 hp Wright engine. It was designed and built in sixty days for Lindbergh and was flown only by the pilot. Fully loaded, the top speed was 124 mph (200 kph). The aircraft is on permanent exhibit at the Smithsonian Institution in Washington, D.C. (Wingspan, 46 feet [14 m]; length, 27 feet 5 inches [8 m].)

**The *Spirit of St. Louis***

# S

**SAILPLANE.** An airplane that flies without an engine. A sailplane flies by gliding downward, but the angle of descent is so small that it can travel many, many miles without any large loss of altitude. It gains height by riding on rising currents of warm air.

Most sailplanes are launched from a hilltop, are towed by an automobile, or are towed by an airplane. The pilot then controls the flight as he or she would control a powered aircraft. Most sailplanes fly at about 50 mph (80 kph), but some can reach speeds of up to 150 mph (241 kph). The altitude record is nearly 9 miles (14 km). The longest flight on record is 908 miles (1,461 km).

The first sailplane was built by Sir George Cayley in England in 1810, but it could fly only a few yards. Otto Lilienthal built and flew the first successful sailplanes in Germany during the 1890s. In 1911, Orville Wright stayed aloft ten minutes in a sailplane. During World War II sailplanes found some use carrying troops and materiel. Often they were towed through the air like railway cars pulled by a locomotive. Today sailplanes are used mostly for sport and recreation.

There is some confusion about the difference between gliders and sailplanes. Most people say they are the same. Some make a distinction, saying that the smaller, simpler craft are gliders, and the larger, better-built ones are sailplanes.

**SAINT-EXUPÉRY, ANTOINE DE** (1900–1944). A French aviation pioneer, as well as a respected writer. His flying career spanned the period from 1922 to 1944, during which time he flew everything from mail planes to newly designed aircraft for test flights. His books are well known for their descriptions of the adventure and heroism of flying.

**SAVOIA-MARCHETTI S-55.** This 1924 aircraft was originally designed as a twin-engine, twin-hull torpedo bomber, but some commercial versions of the plane were made for peacetime use. In 1933 twenty-four Sovoia-Marchetti S-55s left Orbetello, Italy, for the most historic formation flight via Iceland, Greenland, and Labrador to the Century of Progress Exposition in Chicago. The large formation was led by General Italo Balbo, whose name is now used to refer to any large formation. (Wingspan, 79 feet 11 inches [24 m]; length, 54 feet 2 inches [17 m].)

**SEAPLANE.** A plane that can take off from and land on water. Seaplanes can be divided into three groups. Flying boats touch the water with the fuselage of the plane. Floatplanes have pontoons beneath the wings or fuselage, and these are the only parts of the aircraft that touch the water. Amphibians are like flying boats, but they also have landing gear, so they can operate on land or sea.

**A Navy seaplane of the 1920s**

In the 1920s and the 1930s, seaplanes were among the leading aircraft being made. Since then, land-based planes have become more popular. The main use of seaplanes today is to serve as floatplanes in wilderness areas where bodies of water are the only possible landing sites.

**SIKORSKY, IGOR** (1889–1972). A Russian-born aircraft designer. Sikorsky designed and built the world's first four-engine airplane, which he personally flew in 1913. Sikorsky came to America in 1919, where he designed and constructed the first successful single-rotor helicopter in 1939. The Sikorsky helicopter is considered the forerunner of all modern rotary-wing aircraft.

**SIKORSKY ILYA MOUROMETZ.** This Russian large bomber was, in 1914, among the first four-engine bombers ever built. By 1917 about eighty Ilya Mourometz bombers had been constructed. They had four engines and a top speed of 75 mph (120 kph), and they could carry more than 1,500 pounds (680 kg) of bombs and deliver them with pinpoint accuracy. The plane had up to seven machine guns as defense against fighters. In some four hundred bombing raids only one Ilya Mourometz was ever shot down, and that was only after it had destroyed three attacking German fighters. (Wingspan, 101 feet 6 inches [31 m]; length, 65 feet 8 inches [20 m].)

**SIKORSKY S-42.** The transocean flying boat produced in 1934 for Pan American Airways. Sikorsky considered the successful flights of the S-42 across both major oceans as the climax of the pioneering period of aviation.

The S-42 was a large aircraft with the power supplied by four engines which were mounted side by side on the wing's leading edge. The wing and tail were metal and covered with fabric. The plane had seats for thirty-two passengers and carried a four- to five-person crew. On August 16, 1934, the S-42 entered service on the route between Miami and Rio de Janeiro. (Wingspan, 114 feet 2 inches [35 m]; length, 67 feet 8 inches [21 m].)

**SIKORSKY S-60 and S-64 SKYCRANE.** Two helicopters, developed in 1959 and 1962. The S-60 is a massive, heavy-lift aircraft. The S-64, a further development, is designed for military transport duties and has interchangeable "pods" that adapt it for use as a sixty-seven person troop transport, mine sweeper, cargo or missile transport, or for antisubmarine or field-hospital use. These helicopters require a crew of three and have a top forward speed of 127 mph (204 kph).

**SONIC BOOM.** A sound produced by aircraft that fly faster than the speed of sound. At speeds above Mach 1, the plane produces shock waves that move in front of it. These shock waves can be heard on the ground as a sonic boom. The shock waves can cause damage to buildings. Aircraft, such as the Concorde, that fly faster than the speed of sound are called supersonic. Because of the sonic boom, supersonic planes do not fly at speeds faster than sound over populated areas.

**SOPWITH CAMEL.** A famous British attack plane used in World War I. The 1919 aircraft carried twin machine guns that were synchronized to fire together. Powered by either a 110 hp Rhone engine or a 130 hp Clerget engine, these propeller planes had a top speed of 118 mph (189 kph). Captain John Trollope of the British Royal Air Force, flying a Sopwith Camel, shot down a record six German aircraft on a single day, March 25, 1918. (Wingspan, 28 feet [9 m]; length, 18 feet 9 inches [6 m].)

**A Sopwith Camel**

**SPAD 18 CA.** The French biplane fighter, made in 1914, which was one of the most successful aircraft of World War I and a leading plane used in combat. Earlier aircraft were used only for reconnaissance. But then they began to carry gunners and pilots for strafing and aerial bombing. Dogfights, or aerial battles between two or more fighters, became common. (Wingspan, 32 feet 10 inches [10 m]; length, 24 feet 1 inch [7 m].)

**SPIRIT OF ST. LOUIS.** *See* RYAN SPIRIT OF ST. LOUIS.

**SST (SUPERSONIC TRANSPORT).** An airliner that flies faster than the speed of sound. The two SSTs in use today are the BAC-AÉROSPATIALE CONCORDE and the Russian Tu 144. Both fly at about 1,400 mph (2,253 kph). There is some question of whether the construction of SSTs will be stopped until environmental problems, such as noise pollution and damage to the protective ozone in the atmosphere, are solved.

**STOL (*SHORT TAKEOFF* AND *LANDING*).** Aircraft designed to fly from extremely short runways. STOL aircraft are fitted with either a very large wing area or more powerful engines, or they may have other mechanical devices that provide a special high lift to the plane. STOLs are used where long runways are not available.

**STRATOSPHERE.** The layer of the earth's atmosphere above the lowest layer, which is the troposphere. The stratosphere extends from a height of about 6 miles (10 km) to 30 miles (48 km) and offers several advantages over the troposphere for aircraft. There are none of the turbulent weather conditions found lower, so flights are smoother. The air is less dense, creating less resistance to the plane's movement. With thinner air, less oxygen enters the engine, so less fuel is burned. And, finally, the west-to-east jet stream in the stratosphere helps planes flying in that direction.

**SUD-AVIATION CARAVELLE.** A French airliner introduced in 1955. The Caravelle was the first jet aircraft to enter commercial service in the United States. Its two Avon jets are located on the sides of the fuselage, just in front of the tail. Caravelles can carry up to 140 passengers for medium-length runs, and some are still in service with airlines all over the world. (Wingspan, 112 feet 6 inches [34 m]; length, 108 feet 4 inches [33 m].)

**SUKHOI, PAUL OSIPOVICH** (1895–1975). A leading Russian aircraft designer. In 1933 Sukhoi built the first Russian fighter with an enclosed cockpit and retractable landing gear. Beginning in 1936, Sukhoi designed a series of bombers, fighters, and attack planes, all identified by the prefix Su.

**SUPERMARINE SPITFIRE.** The best-known British combat plane of World War II. All in all, twenty-four different types of Spitfires were made, starting in 1936, for a total production run of more than twenty thousand aircraft. While the early Spitfires had a speed of 365 mph (587 kph), the final Mark 24 could reach 450 mph (724 kph). The various models were armed with different combinations of machine guns and cannon. (Wingspan, 36 feet 10 inches [11 m]; length, 29 feet 11 inches [9 m].)

**SUPERSONIC FLIGHT.** Aircraft flight at speeds beyond the speed of sound. The speed of sound varies with altitude. At sea level it is about 760 mph (1,223 kph). At an altitude of 7 miles (11 km), it drops to 660 mph (1,062 kph). The speed of sound is often referred to a Mach 1. If a plane reaches a speed beyond Mach 1, it achieves supersonic flight. The first supersonic flight was in a rocket-powered Bell X-1 in 1947. The first jet plane to attain supersonic speed was a Douglas Skyrocket in 1949. The current speed record of more than Mach 3 was established in 1976 in a Lockheed SR-71.

**SWING WING.** A design which permits the aircraft to change its wing shape in flight. For takeoff, landing, and slow-speed flight, the wings are moved into a straight-wing shape for greater lift. For high-speed flight, the wings are moved back to give a swept-wing or delta-wing shape, which cuts down drag. The British scientist Dr. Barnes Wallis designed, but never built, the first swing-wing aircraft, called the *Swallow*. Later, swing-wing planes were built in the United States and became an important part of combat-plane design.

**United States Air Force F-111A swing wing aircraft**

# T

**TAIL.** The rear section of a plane. The tail contains the upright fin or vertical stabilizer. The rear part of the fin is the movable rudder, which controls turns to the right or left. The tailplane or horizontal stabilizer is also part of the tail. The rear part of the tailplane is the hinged elevator, which controls diving and climbing.

**TANKERS.** Planes that carry fuel for other aircraft and are able to refuel fighters and bombers while in the air. This gives such military planes an almost unlimited range.

**TAYLOR CUB.** One of the best-known light monoplanes of all time. The craft was produced from 1931 until 1950. The name was changed to Piper Cub in 1937 after William T. Piper bought the manufacturing plant. During that period, 23,512 Cubs were built; many are still in use to this day. (Wingspan, 35 feet 2 inches [11 m]; length, 22 feet 6 inches [7 m].)

**TEST PILOT.** A highly skilled pilot specially trained to handle emergencies. Test pilots are the first to fly newly designed planes. They also test fly production planes before delivery to customers. The test pilots check the safety of the planes and make sure they meet the design requirements.

**THRUST.** The force produced by a jet or rocket engine that drives an aircraft forward. These engines burn a fuel in a combustion chamber, giving off an exhaust of hot gases. The gases rushing out through the rear of the engine do not provide the thrust. Rather, it is the pressure of the gases inside pushing forward on the front wall of the engine. Thrust is usually measured in pounds (lbs) or kilograms (kgs).

**TRAINERS.** Special aircraft used to train crews in their operation.

**TRANSPORT.** An airplane which is built to carry cargo or people from one place to another.

**TRIDENT.** *See* HAWKER SIDDELEY TRIDENT.

**TRIM.** Adjusting small flaps in the fin and wings to keep the plane at the right altitude, without pitching or rolling.

**TRIPLANE.** An aircraft with three sets of wings, one above the other. The German air ace of World War I, "Red Baron" (Manfred von Richthofen), flew a Fokker Triplane. By 1918 interest in triplanes waned.

**TUPOLEV, ANDREI NIKOLAEVICH** (1888–1972). An outstanding Russian aircraft designer. He planned a number of heavy bombers for Russia during World War II. His Tu-20 bomber and Tu-114 airliner were the world's fastest propeller planes. The Tu-144 was the first supersonic airliner to be flown.

**TUPOLEV TU-144.** The Russian supersonic airliner which made its maiden flight in 1968, more than two months before the British-French supersonic Concorde. Like the somewhat smaller Concorde, the Tu-144 has delta wings and a downward pointing nose. It is powered for Mach 2.4 top speed by four Kuznetsov jet engines, each producing a thrust of 44,090 pounds (20,000 kg). The Tu-144 seats 140 passengers and has a 4,560-mile (7,337-km) range. The greatest altitude of the Tu-144 is 65,000 feet (19,812 m). (Wingspan, 94 feet 10 inches [29 m]; length, 212 feet 7 inches [65 m].)

**TURBOJET ENGINE.** A jet engine that compresses the incoming air, which is then mixed with the fuel and burned in the combustion chamber. The burning mixtures create gases that give the engine its thrust.

**TURBOPROP ENGINE.** A special kind of engine in which fuel is burned in a combustion chamber, and the exhaust gases are used to drive a propeller. Turboprop engines are used in some VTOLs and some helicopters.

**TWA.** A large American airline, originally known as Transcontinental and Western Air, Inc. Formed on July 16, 1930, TWA (TransWorld Airlines) began coast-to-coast service on October 25 of that year. During World War II TWA flew transatlantic military flights, and it started commercial operations to London on February 5, 1946. Today the airline's routes cover the United States, Europe, Africa, and the Orient.

**U-2.** *See* LOCKHEED U-2.

**UNDERCARRIAGE.** The landing gear of an aircraft. The undercarriage is usually pulled back into the wings and fuselage during flight.

**UNITED AIR LINES.** The world's largest privately owned airline. Formed in 1931, United Air Lines' routes cover the United States, including Hawaii, as well as Canada and Mexico.

**U.S. AIR FORCE.** In 1907 the U.S. Army set up an Aeronautical Division to study the possible uses of "flying machines." Before the United States entered World War I in 1917, there was little use for military aircraft. Soon, though, planes began to be used for scouting, bombing, and to attack enemy aircraft.

After the war, there were many advances in civilian aviation, but little interest was shown in developing military planes. Brig. Gen. William "Billy" Mitchell, Chief of the Air Service of the Army, was court-martialed for his outspoken insistence on the importance of military aviation.

During the United States' involvement in World War II (1941–1945) the air operations of both the Army and the Navy were organized as independent commands. At top strength, the Army Air Forces had nearly 2.5 million men and 80,000 planes. After the war, on September 18, 1947, Congress created the U.S. Air Force as an equal partner to the Army and Navy.

The Air Force is divided into four commands. The Strategic Air Command controls the bombing and reconnaissance operations. The Tactical Air Command provides air support for Army and Navy forces. The Air Defense Command is responsible for protection against enemy attack. And the Space Command is in charge of all military operations in space.

**VICKERS VC-10.** Built in Britain in 1962, the VC-10 is a popular long-range jet airliner. Its four jets are mounted at the rear of the fuselage, two on each side. The tail has a distinctive high T-shape. An improved model, the Super VC-10, has four Conway jets, each giving 22,500 pounds (10,205 kg) of thrust, and a speed of about 580 mph (930 kph). It can transport about 180 passengers for distances of up to 7,128 miles (11,450 km). (Wingspan, 146 feet 2 inches [45 m]; length, 171 feet 8 inches [52 m]).

**VOISIN BIPLANE.** One of the first examples of a pusher biplane, with forward elevator and rudder in the tail, built in 1907 by the Voisin brothers, Gabriel and Charles. Frenchman Henri Farman flew a Voisin 3,380 feet (1,030 m) in 1 minute and 14 seconds. It was the first time an airplane, other than the Wrights', had stayed in the air for more than one minute. (Wingspan, 33 feet 6 inches [10 m].)

**The Voisin-Delagrange I, piloted by Charles Voisin**

**VOISIN BOMBER.** This aircraft, derived from the biplane of 1907, had a metal structure and a remarkably powerful engine. Fitted with a heavy Hotchkiss rifle-caliber machine gun, a Voisin Bomber won the first combat engagement with an enemy aircraft, on October 5, 1914. The plane had a maximum speed of 84 mph (135 kph) and a range of 311 miles (500 km). (Wingspan, 48 feet 4 inches [15 m]; length, 31 feet 3 inches [10 m].)

**VTOL (Vertical Takeoff and Landing).** An aircraft that can fly straight up into the air. The helicopter is an example of a VTOL aircraft. Because of the helicopter's limited speed, though, considerable research is being done to develiop a fixed-wing VTOL craft.

A number of different approaches to VTOL are being studied. Some of the possibilities are deflecting the thrust of the jet engines to move the plane in a vertical direction, using separate engines for flight and for takeoff and landing, rotating the engines themselves, tilting the entire wing, and designing planes to take off from a tail-down position. The first method, called vectored thrust, has proved most practical. In the late 1960s, the British Harrier became the first operational VTOL fighter.

**A USAF X-13 Vertijet, a VTOL research plane tested in 1957**

**WAL.** *See* DORNIER DO J WAL.

**WIND TUNNEL.** A tunnellike passage through which air is forced by powerful fans. Wind tunnels are used to make aerodynamic measurements on new aircraft designs. Since a full-size plane is too large to fit into most wind tunnels, a smaller model of the craft is usually used.

**WINGS.** The parts of the plane that extend out from the fuselage and that provide the aircraft's lift. When a plane begins to move, air flows over the wings. The upper surfaces of the wings are curved upward, while the lower surfaces are basically flat. Because of the curve, the air moves faster over the wing tops. Air that is moving at high speed, according to Bernoulli's Principle, has less pressure than slower-moving air. Therefore, there is less pressure above the wings than below. This causes the craft to rise up off the ground and into the air.

**WING SPAN.** The distance from one wing tip to the other. It includes the width of the plane's fuselage.

**WORLD CRUISER.** *See* DOUGLAS WORLD CRUISERS.

**WRIGHT BROTHERS, ORVILLE** (1871–1948) **and WILBUR** (1867–1912). Bicycle makers from Dayton, Ohio, who invented and built the first successful power-driven, heavier-than-air aircraft. The brothers became interested in flying around 1896. From 1900 to 1902 they experimented on a strip of sand at Kitty Hawk, North Carolina, with their first man-carrying glider. With the glider they worked out most of the problems of balance in flight. Plans for a power airplane began in 1902. By the fall of 1903, they had completed the *Flyer* and on December 17, 1903, they made the first flight at Kitty Hawk, ushering in the air age.

**WRIGHT FLYER.** The first power plane built and flown by the Wright brothers. On December 17, 1903, at Kitty Hawk, North Carolina, the brothers made the first attempts to fly the *Flyer* with engine power alone. Orville took the first turn. After a 40-foot (12-m) run on the catapult rail, he flew about 10 feet (3.05 m) off the ground for a distance of 120 feet (37 m) and landed safely twelve seconds later. Three more flights were made the same day. The longest was 825 feet (260 m) and lasted fifty-nine seconds.

Power to drive the two propellers came from a 12 hp engine via bicycle chains. To control the *Flyer* in flight, the Wrights devised a system of twisting the wing tips. When one end of the wing was raised the other end lowered. The aircraft turned in the direction of the lower wing tip. The twisting was done by cables running to levers set beside the pilot.

The *Flyer* was built for less than $1,000 and weighed about 750 pounds (340 kg), including the pilot. The biplane can be seen on exhibit at the Smithsonian Institute in Washington, D.C. (Wingspan, 40 feet 4 inches [12 m]; length, 21 feet 1 inch [6 m].)

**The Wright *Flyer***

# X-Y-Z

**X-1.** *See* BELL X-1.
**X-15.** *See* NORTH AMERICAN X-15.

**YAW.** One of the three basic movements of an aircraft. Yaw refers to turning toward the right or left while in flight. *See also* PITCH and ROLL.

**ZEPPELIN.** *See* AIRSHIP and DIRIGIBLE.

**ZEPPELIN, FERDINAND VON** (1838–1917). A German designer of airships. These vehicles, or zeppelins, were gas-filled bags that were powered and controlled by engines. They were used in night raids against Great Britain during World War I. Because of this, they are notorious for taking part in the first planned air raids against civilians in history. As soon as British fighter planes that could climb higher came into use, the airship became obsolete for military purposes.

Ferdinand von Zeppelin had first become interested in lighter-than-air craft after he visited the United States during the Civil War and observed the Union Army's use of balloons to scan enemy positions and direct cannon fire. His first rigid metal framework dirigible made its maiden flight on July 2, 1900.